Coal Miners' Wives

COAL MINERS' WIVES

Portraits of Endurance

CAROL A. B. GIESEN

THE UNIVERSITY PRESS OF KENTUCKY

Copyright © 1995 by The University Press of Kentucky

Scholarly publisher for the Commonwealth,
serving Bellarmine College, Berea College, Centre
College of Kentucky, Eastern Kentucky University,
The Filson Club, Georgetown College, Kentucky
Historical Society, Kentucky State University,
Morehead State University, Murray State University,
Northern Kentucky University, Transylvania University,
University of Kentucky, University of Louisville,
and Western Kentucky University.

Editorial and Sales Offices: Lexington, Kentucky 40508-4008

Library of Congress Cataloging-in-Publication Data

Giesen, Carol A. B., 1931–
    Coal miners' wives : portraits of endurance / Carol A.B. Giesen.
        p.   cm.
    Includes bibliographical references and index.
    ISBN 0-8131-1903-0
    1. Coal miners' spouses—West Virginia.   2. Women—West Virginia
—Social conditions.   I. Title.
HD8039.M62U6253   1995
305.42'09754—dc20   94-37966

Contents

Illustrations follow page   68

Tables

Preface

In 1978 I became acquainted with a neighbor whose husband was employed as a roof bolter in the nearby mine. Her friendship and her comments on her life led me to develop a research project on the daily lives of women married to miners. I eventually completed the research and, under the pressure of other events, laid it aside. In 1985 current work with women who were coping with other kinds of stress brought my attention back to the interviews with miners' wives, and I reestablished contact with some of the original interviewees.

I also began to search for general information on women in mining families, but, to my dismay, there appeared to be very little information available on the conditions of their lives or their families. The most frequent responses I received from reference librarians, historians, and database directors were requests for me to share what I found with them.

As the search broadened over time, I turned to edited books of anecdotes, stories of people's lives, history texts, journals on Appalachian life, and even movies. These sources were invaluable, and I obtained much of the background information for this book from them. However, the majority of the content of the book came directly from the interviews. To protect the women's identities and those of their families, I gave each woman a pseudonym and summarized ideas, comments, and problems mentioned by more than one woman.

I have made no attempt to present a precise scientific analysis of the stresses and strains of their lives or the efficacy of their coping methods. Over the past several decades, psychologists and sociologists have carried out numerous thorough quantitative research studies to investigate stress and coping. The products of these studies are enormously valuable in understanding how human beings structure their perceptions of an often troublesome world and create useful strategies to cope with life events. In this book, however, I present a subjective view through the use of naturalistic methods and after the manner of ethnographic "realist tales" (Van Maanen 1988, 49).

Finally, I wish to express my deepest appreciation to the eighteen women who shared their lives with me and my gratitude to the people who helped by providing useful criticisms, guidance, and patient support.

Coal Miners' Wives

ONE

Raising Consciousness: An Overview

It's midmorning when the sirens sound, but in minutes people are gathering outside the tall wire fence. Others are on their way, and in homes out of reach of the sirens' sounds, telephones are ringing. From the distance, other sirens begin, shrill pulses that grow steadily nearer. Twenty minutes later, a hundred people stand outside the fence, and the number grows quickly.

The crowd is subdued, waiting. Most are women. Some are crying, while others try to comfort them. Some are praying aloud; others hold themselves tightly with folded arms and pray silently. The look of fear is on everyone's face; the sound of sobbing draws some near and pushes others away.

The big gates stay closed. Inside the fence there is more activity. The people outside can see men working frantically to organize and carry out a rescue. Others inside stand in silent groups of two or three, smoking cigarettes, watching the pit mouth, talking about what may have happened, to whom, and why. The more experienced people inside and outside the fence have lived through this before. They talk of other times, other accidents. The less experienced among them have heard it all before from fathers or mothers, grandparents or friends; but for some of them, it has never been real until now. They wait, shuffling their feet and talking nervously.

The greatest fear of the women outside the fence has leaped into shocking reality. No one outside knows who is in danger or what has happened, but they know the dangers that exist and the frightening possibilities. Somewhere deep under the ground men and women may be choking in blinding dust; they may be crushed, burned, or electrocuted. Husbands, fathers, brothers, or sons may be brought out crushed, torn, or burned. The victims may be their mothers, sisters, aunts, or friends. The waiting women do not know which of them will go home with their loved ones at their side and which of them will go to the hospital to wait and pray. They know the chances are great that some will go home in shock and disbelief at the death of someone they love.

If another accident happens tomorrow, next week, next month, or in any of the coming years, you will see many of the same faces outside the gate with the same tightly controlled look. The threat of death does not occur occasionally in mining families. It is a daily threat that pervades the lives of those whose family members and neighbors work in the deep coal mines of West Virginia.

The threats of death and injury to loved ones are not the only threats to the welfare of these West Virginia families. There are also frequent strikes, layoffs, and the seemingly inevitable black lung. There is the threat of finding no work for themselves when mining spouses are unemployed, no means of putting food on the table for their families, of having to depend on others or on welfare. There is also a pervasive underlying sense of resentment and hostility for the uncaring attitude of coal company policies and regulatory bodies that fail to carry out their responsibilities.

Who are the people who wait outside the coal company fences and why do they choose to live their lives in an environment in which death, injury, and unemployment are frequent realities? How do they manage their daily lives in the face of such threatening events? How do they prepare themselves to deal with these realities and how well do they cope? The answers to these questions lie partially in the stories of their individual lives, in their shared cultural and social heritage, and in family traditions. Some answers seem apparent in the economy of West Virginia and the central role of mining to that economy. A greater part of the answers, however, is found in the human spirit, strength, flexibility, and endurance of the people themselves.

A little over a decade ago, I was first given the opportunity to spend many hours in conversation with a group of women who taught me about the strength and endurance that women possess in adverse circumstances. As the child of a middle-class, white-collar family with parents and adult relatives raised on farms and ranches, I had heard tales of the dangers and strains that farm families sometimes experience. On the other hand, the major problems with which my immediate family had to cope tended to arise from marital strains and the everyday tensions all families experience. Nothing in my background prepared me to understand that in some families death or serious injury is a daily threat.

Late in my career, I began graduate work at West Virginia University. Through my acquaintance with a neighbor whose husband was a roof bolter in a nearby coal mine, I became aware for the first time of the intensity and constancy of the stresses that impact on some women and their families. As we became friends, I began to learn about the life of a miner's wife. She spoke of the anxieties she felt when her husband was late coming home from work and the strain of being both mother and father in order to relieve her husband of some home responsibilities. She made a daily effort to keep things at home running smoothly so he would not worry while working and perhaps cause an accident through inattentiveness. And occasionally she had to struggle to keep the family finances at an adequate level through unexpected times of no employment.

Knowledge of the nature of deep-mine coal mining compounded and intensified these stresses and strains. Both my friend and her husband were from mining families, and both had lost family members in the mines over the years. In their social network, death was familiar. Many had experienced major but not disabling injuries, and plaguing problems such as persistent limb, joint, or back ailments were commonplace. The threat of black lung was felt by every family. The hazards of mining and their consequences were a part of their daily lives.

I learned that my friend and other women she knew believed that the miners felt less anxiety and worry about the dangers of mining than their wives because the miners encountered the dangers daily and used direct and active methods to increase their safety. The miners themselves learned the skills of their jobs, exercised caution, and relied on their fellow workers and supervisors to inform them and give help when necessary. The miners' wives, on the other hand, could do little to make their husbands safer, and their helplessness created anxiety and worry. It was the miner's wife (and in contemporary times, the miner's husband) who waited at home for a spouse to return. My friend told me that the men faced the dangers every day but that it was the women who "carried the mine in them."

As our acquaintance grew, I became curious about how the miners' wives coped with the persistent stress of anxiety and worry. My neighbor believed she coped fairly effectively even though she experienced sleep disturbances, days of poor appetite, short but fairly regular periods of depression, and the sense of foreboding that typifies anxiety. She envied women who could cope with their anxieties more successfully than she. There were such women, she assured me, although she did not know any of them personally.

My curiosity continued to grow as I met other women whose husbands worked in the mines. How did other women cope with such stressful circumstances? What did they do that my neighbor did not do, and were their coping methods more successful? It seemed unlikely that there were any "sure-cure" methods to reduce the stress of knowing that someone you love works in conditions in which death or serious injury happens frequently. Nevertheless, if some miners' wives were not bothered by anxiety over the dangers of their husbands' occupations, finding out how they managed to avoid it seemed important.

Other concerns also surfaced in our conversations. My neighbor talked about the constraints placed on family hopes and plans by the knowledge that the family income could (and did) disappear repeatedly without warning and for unpredictable lengths of time. She spoke of the anger she felt because the coal companies seemed neither to know nor to care about the lives and welfare of the people who made it possible for the companies to become wealthy and powerful. She explained why she believed that politicians, regulatory groups, and even unions all played a part in creating and maintaining oppressive and harmful working conditions and how that belief made it difficult for her to feel optimistic about her life.

My interest in understanding how the daily conditions and experience of people's lives influenced their growth and development became focused on understanding how miners' wives managed to survive under such stresses. I asked my neighbor if she would help me make contacts with other miners' wives, and, with her help, I began to meet and talk to other women. Her friends were immediately interested, and each helped me develop a network of miners' wives of various ages. Each woman with whom I talked contacted another miners wife and explained my interest. If the new person was also interested, we would discuss over the telephone the issues I wished to raise and then make arrangements to meet and talk. In this way, each woman began her face-to-face conversations with me after a background talk with a friend and a preliminary phone conversation with me. As the network grew, another woman trained in interviewing began to assist in contacting and talking to the wives of miners.

The few issues my neighbor and I discussed initially focused on how she coped with her anxieties. As the network of miners' wives expanded, it became clear that the conditions of their husbands' employment touched nearly all aspects of their lives. After a great deal of thought and discussion with the several women who had been my first contacts, I developed an interview schedule that became the vehicle for the later conversations with other miners' wives. The interview schedule was a series of open-ended questions about worry and conflicts, events that create tension and anxiety, coping, and learning to cope (see Appendix D).

A few other issues were also included. Because the women often mentioned beliefs about fate and God's role in determining the events in people's lives, the subjects of fate, God's will,

and determination in general became a part of our conversations. Near the end of our talks, I asked the women to give
their predictions for themselves and their families and to fur-
nish background information on themselves, their husbands,
and their families. Finally, I asked if they wished to discuss any
other issues or to give other kinds of information about themselves. Their responses to these questions often included
women's issues, political views, and comments on the local
educational institutions. My assistant and I tape-recorded for
later transcription all of our conversations except the more
random and broadly ranging postinterview discussions.

A year after we began talking to miners' wives and nearly a
year and a half after my first conversation with my neighbor
about mining and miners' wives, we had collected hours of tape-
recorded discussions with women ranging in age from the early
twenties to the late sixties. About half were under and half were
over forty years old. The condensing of the interviews showed,
in general terms, the interrelationships of gender roles, the traditions of mining families, and the structure and conditions of
their husbands' occupation (see Appendix C). Although we
could not precisely define such complex relationships with our
naturalistic methods, the women's descriptions of their experiences spoke quite clearly of the meaning of such relationships.

In the next few pages, an overview of our conversations
briefly introduces the women, the issues they believed were
most problematic in their lives, and their methods of coping.
Most of these issues are then presented in the remaining chapters as the women described them. A following section makes
some comparisons between miners' wives and women married
to men in other high-risk occupations such as police work,
active military duty, and commercial crabbing, oystering, and
fishing (see Appendix B). In general, however, such comparisons
are few and difficult to make because very little has been done
to investigate the stresses that women and families experience
when husbands and fathers are engaged in hazardous occupations.

My neighbor told me that West Virginians, in contrast to the
historically mobile American family, tended to stay in West

Virginia and not move far from home. Her words were true for all but two of the women in a group that eventually included eighteen women. Two of the women were born outside the state and moved to West Virginia as young children. The other women were born and raised within fifty miles of their present homes. At the time of our talks, most of the wives lived within five to fifteen miles of their childhood homes.

West Virginia was home to the parents and grandparents of most of the women as well. The young men the interviewees grew up with or met as young adults were also likely to have been born and raised in West Virginia. During the years the women were growing to adulthood, many of the men they knew went into the mines to work. Few other types of employment that paid wages sufficient to support a family were available in their home areas, and, as my neighbor said, West Virginians tend to stay close to home.

All were young when they married their miner husbands. Some were only sixteen or seventeen, and one married at fifteen. One woman lost her husband in the mines after only a few years of marriage and was just twenty when she married another miner. Families were very important to these young women and their husbands, and, in most of their families, the first child came along within a year or two after they married. At the time of our conversations, their children's ages ranged from infancy to adulthood, and many of the middle-aged and older women had grandchildren. The oldest woman had great-grandchildren.

For nearly all of the middle-aged and older women, marrying young had meant dropping out of school. All but two of the younger women, however, had completed high school before marriage, and one young woman had gone to college for two years. In general, the women's husbands had had fewer years of education than their wives because many of the men had left school at a young age to go to work in the mines. Some of the older men had entered the mines as young as ten or eleven years old. Although more of the younger men than the older men had completed high school, the availability of mining jobs had persuaded many to drop out in the ninth or tenth grade to go to work.

Raising a family was expensive, and miners' wages often needed to be supplemented by additional income. The older women, in particular, had married and started families during years when the wages paid were not sufficient to support a family. However, for younger and older women alike, combining homemaking and outside employment was a common experience. Those who were willing to work at full time jobs continuously, rather than for temporary periods, were more likely to be able to find jobs paying more than minimum wages. Those who wished to work only when extra money was needed nearly always found only low paying work.

Finding any work was seldom easy, and over the years most of the women worked at jobs ranging from cleaning houses to clerical work. The times when they needed money to supplement or replace their husbands' incomes, such as during a strike or layoff, were also times when more women or men were looking for jobs. In addition, employers were sometimes reluctant to hire women who would leave the job after the family finances had improved. Few of the women had occupational skills that qualified them, even in the best of times, for work other than relatively low-wage jobs with few or no opportunities for advancement or wage increases.

Regardless of whether they worked full or part time, temporarily or continuously, all of the women considered themselves full-time homemakers. Fulfilling the traditional homemaker's role gave them feelings of pride in themselves as well as expressed the support they gave to their husbands. They saw dual roles of homemaker-wage earner as necessary and desirable to maintain the family. Wage earning provided additional needed money for the household or for themselves. Good homemaking provided material and emotional support for children and relieved husbands of having to carry concerns about home down into the mines.

When the women talked about the problems they experienced at home and the things that caused them to worry, shift work was always at the top or near the top of their lists. They usually named the dangers of mining, and mine strikes and layoffs as the second or third causes of worry. Nearly everyone believed that shift work, strikes, or layoffs made the normally dangerous working conditions even more dangerous. It was often the fatigue, they said, that occurred when changing shifts or beginning new shifts at the end of a strike or layoff that caused accidents.

Shift work, however, caused many other problems for the miners' wives and families. The women recounted multiple family and home problems stemming from their husbands' changing times for work, sleep, and waking activity. All of the family's activities from weekly shopping to the couple's intimate relations were affected by the lack of a consistent schedule. Family chores that in most families are done by husbands were done by the women or postponed until weekends or vacation times. Normal daytime homemaking activities such as cleaning or laundry often had to be done at odd hours in order to make the home quieter when husbands were sleeping during the day. Women with younger children worried about the absence of husbands during night hours, worry that was increased by their husbands' inaccessibility while at work.

Tension and conflict between couples sometimes arose from the miners' lack of time for discussing family problems or planning family activities. The fatigue often experienced by the miners when they changed from one shift to another was likely to add to these problems because it created irritation or an unwillingness to invest emotional energy in family problem solving. Some of the women felt anger when problems could not or would not be discussed in a timely fashion, but others felt torn between wishing to spare their husbands from undue concern over family problems and feeling deprived of their partners' input.

Social contacts also suffered from the miners' shift work, and some women felt their husbands' working schedules made it nearly impossible for the family to participate in social contacts with their extended families or with friends. For rural women, in particular, their husbands' lack of time or lack of interest in maintaining social contacts increased feelings of isolation. For some women, loneliness became a frequent problem, and, for a few younger women, it became a serious problem with periods of depression, crying spells, feelings of loneliness, and difficulty in continuing normal marital relations.

Although the first problems mentioned in relation to husbands' jobs were usually problems caused by shift work, the next problems mentioned were nearly always the persistent worry and anxiety caused by the dangers of mining. More than half of the women believed they worried about their husbands nearly all of the time the men were down in the mine. The other women felt they worried only some of the time. However, except for one woman, "some of the time" meant frequently occurring specific times such as at the beginning or end of a shift or at the start of a new shift.

Their general sense of worry always heightened when some unusual circumstances occurred. The phone ringing at night when their husbands were at work, hearing the mine siren blow, any delay in their husbands' return from work, or hearing that there had been an accident at the mine increased their tension. Some found it difficult to contain their fears at such times and felt compelled to try to phone the mine or drive there to see if an accident had occurred. Others tried to contain their fears by busying themselves with work or occupying their minds with other thoughts, prayer, or phone calls to friends.

They believed that mining was the most dangerous job a man could have and that much of the stress in their lives arose from their concerns over their husbands' safety. Their knowledge of the dangers of mining came from sources close to them. Deaths or injuries from mine fires, cave-ins, explosions, and electrocution were a part of the experiences of their families, relatives, friends, neighbors, and husbands.

The immediate dangers of mining such as fires and explosions were not the only sources of worry for the miners' wives. They also worried about black lung, the disease that reflects the long-term effects of exposure to sharp-edged particles of dust. Many of the women's older relatives suffered from the disease, and it was common knowledge that even young miners might be affected by black lung. Those who remained in the mines for years were never untouched by the build-up of dust that clogged the lungs and reduced breathing capacity.

The symptoms of stress experienced by the miners' wives ranged from daily, mild levels of irritability to occasional panic attacks. Everyone mentioned periods of feeling sad or "blue," of not being able to control crying spells, or feelings of being trapped in a situation she could not control. Nearly everyone occasionally had insomnia or early waking and loss of appetite either preceding or following some unusual event in the mine. A few women suffered from physical problems such as asthma, hives, and stomach upsets.

When these feelings occurred, the wives sought relief by finding some work or other activity that would keep hands and minds busy. Housework, gardening, hobbies, playing the piano, or concentrating on their work at their places of employment were all ways of suppressing worried thoughts. Many women found it helpful to talk to others, particularly to other miners' wives, parents or siblings, or friends. A few of the women believed that prayer, quiet reflection, or reading the Bible were the most effective ways of coping with worry, but that keeping busy also reduced some of their tension.

Nearly all believed that learning to cope with the stresses of being a miner's wife began with learning to accept the conditions of their husbands' jobs and to rely on themselves to establish daily routines to maintain their families and homes. The women said that no one but a miner's wife could understand the stresses of a miner's wife. Consequently, being able to give support to and receive support from other wives was also important. Many of the women also said they had learned to develop an interest in a hobby, community activities, or church activities to occupy time not spent on family routines. Several young women found it useful to occupy their free time in preparing themselves to continue their education or to begin self-employment.

One of my first and most pressing questions after I had listened to my neighbor's stories was why she and other women did not urge their husbands to take other jobs. If no jobs were available in their immediate home area, why did they not leave the area and find employment elsewhere? My naive assumption, based on my own life and those of others from my social background, was that the search for suitable employment often took people to other towns, other states, or even other countries. True, it would surely be difficult for families and would entail some sacrifices. On the other hand, steady work at a job that did not present daily threats to the worker's life and thereby also endanger the emotional health of the family should take high priority.

My neighbor made it clear to me that these ideas were typical of an outsider. Not many of those who considered themselves West Virginians would choose to abandon their homes and go elsewhere to work merely because mining was, in their opinion, the world's worst work. Later I found these sentiments were shared by other mining families as well. I heard them expressed by other miners' wives, and I read them in accounts of Kentucky miners' wives (Maggard 1990b; Scott 1988). This was home, this was what people did here to earn their living. It was more than just a paying job. The work of mining, its history throughout the West Virginia mountains, and the family lives of coal miners were all parts of a way of life. Many believed it was a way of life that was disappearing but, nevertheless, it was their present way of life.

Central to this way of life was the role of the miners' wives. From the beginning of our talks, the interviewees made clear that they did not believe that the traditional role of women in mining families was a reflection of the stereotype of women as submissive nurturers. They felt they were partners in their husbands' lives in a greater sense. They carried the major share of home and family responsibilities so that their husbands would suffer less fatigue. They adjusted their plans, their decisions, and their family schedules to their husbands' needs, and in other smaller ways tried to send their men free of worry into the mines. This was the tradition of mining wives and mining families.

Most of the women believed that a miner's wife should not have to carry the burdens she did. Some said it was unfair to have to carry the burden of unequal responsibilities, and, in a few families, these convictions were a source of conflict. Nearly all said that the difficulties experienced by mining families were greater than they had expected. Even the women who had been raised in mining families believed it was hard to adjust to the stresses and strains of having a husband working underground. When they were children, their mothers and other adults mediated the fears and tensions that arose from their fathers' occupations. As wives they experienced these emotions directly.

In some mining families, activism in worker-company relations was also a part of women's tradition. Women picketed, marched in demonstrations, lay down in front of trucks, wrote letters, and supported in other ways the workers' and mining union's efforts to change conditions in the mines. I was reminded more than a few times both by their words and by other accounts (Maggard 1990a, 1990b; Scott 1988) that the history of mining throughout Appalachia had been one of frequent strife and that, on at least one occasion, an open shooting war between miners and company men had taken place. Miners' wives, mothers, and other mining-family women actively participated in one role or another in many of these conflicts (Maggard 1990a).

In many respects, the wives' view of women in mining families as activist-supporters reflected the broader actualities of many women's lives across all of the generations of American women. Pioneer women, farm women, and other women married to men in demanding occupations have often carried the major burdens of home and family responsibilities so that the family will survive. Further, when geography, economy, and politics have combined to limit people's lives and welfare, it has often been the wives and mothers in workers' families who have motivated change by rejecting the status quo for their children (Coles 1972; Maggard 1990a; Scott 1988).

However, there was another side to the activist-supporter role espoused by these miners' wives. The other side reflected a fundamental acceptance of men's dominance in regard to the rights of the individuals in a marriage relationship to choose an occupation. They married men who were or became coal miners whether out of preference or because of the availability of work or the level of wages. If the men did not want to leave and work elsewhere, wives and families had no acceptable choice other than to cope with the consequences of the chosen occupation. The women's acceptance was nearly always expressed in the same way—it was a man's right to work where he wished to work.

In the chapters that follow, the West Virginia miners' wives who shared their stories with me describe aspects of their daily lives and their special problems. Other authors have written of the people in the Appalachian coal-mining areas and of the effects on their lives of the unemployment, poor health, and lack of education characteristic of much of this country (see, for example, Coles 1972; Maggard 1990b; and Scott 1988). However, too little attention has been given to the voices of the women in the mining families. They spoke to us clearly and poignantly of their lives, their problems, and their hopes for the future. In the final editing and summarization of their stories, I tried to be a "conduit" for their views and experiences as ethnographer John Van Maanen recommended (1988, 45).

TWO

Traditional Views: The Backgrounds of Their Lives

Most of the eighteen women whose stories make up this book were second, third, or fourth generation West Virginians. Their grandfathers, fathers, and other male ancestors had earned their living, and some had died, in the deep coal mines that were the primary industry of West Virginia. As we sat and talked in their living rooms and kitchens, their husbands, sons, and sons-in-law labored under the mountains to bring out the coal.

The decades between their ancestors' time and contemporary times had brought tremendous change to the mining lands of Appalachia. A few of the traditions and values of earlier generations were weakened or eliminated as social and economic change moved through the hollows and hillsides, but others were supported and strengthened. Among the values and attitudes that remained strong across the years was the importance of home and family as the central structures in the lives of mining families. Indeed, for many, the immediate family was the central point in large and complex extended-family networks.

The advantages of the family network remained significant over the generations. When necessary, the immediate family and relatives living nearby pooled their resources and talents to help the family members survive and, through work and faith, to prosper. As long as these ties were strong, the help that was needed for breaking new land, for building, for healing, and for caring for new families was available. Further, as the children of each generation grew to adulthood, the family was the mechanism through which they learned the necessary

attributes of resourcefulness, independence, and self-suffi-
ciency (Coward and Jackson 1983; Lewis, Kobak, and Johnson
1973).

In the women's families, as in previous generations, the
family was the center of the social support network (Althouse
1974; Appalachian Consortium 1981; Scott 1988); and it was
comforting to have relatives near. The few women whose families lived more than a few miles away would have liked them
to have been closer. They felt that family could be relied upon
in times when neighbors, friends, and others might not be
willing to help. Even when there were disagreements or tensions between family members, family could be counted on. As
one woman said, "They might not like something you did or
disagree with you about something, but when you need your
family to help, you got the feeling those things don't matter."
Younger women said they had looked to their mothers, aunts,
and sometimes even grandmothers to help them learn to cope
with problems. Older women recalled the many times when
their families had been the only buffer between misfortune and
deprivation.

The extended family was also a primary source of social
interactions that ranged from the most casual telephone chats
and grocery-shopping trips to regular participation in weekly
activities and family camping trips. These social relationships
with parents, in-laws, siblings, and other relatives were secondary in importance only to relationships with husbands, wives,
and children. The importance and meaning of these family ties
kept many mining families from leaving to make their living in
other locations (Althouse 1974; Lewis, Kobak, and Johnson
1973; Scott 1988).

The desire to remain close to relatives meant that the families of the women we interviewed had moved little, and most
of the women still lived close to their parents, siblings, or other
relatives. Only two had ever lived more than fifty miles away
from their present homes. One was born just across the West
Virginia state line in Pennsylvania, although her family moved
to a mining community while she was still an infant. The

mining community no longer existed as a community, but her present home was only a few miles away from her childhood home. Another woman had come to West Virginia from Texas when she was a child, and neither she nor her family had traveled away from their West Virginia home since that time.

Nancy's description of her family relationships was typical of many of the other women both in West Virginia and in other Appalachian mining areas (Scott 1988). She had been born and grew to adulthood just a few miles away from the neighborhood where she lived as a miner's wife. She said she felt as though she knew most of the local people in her small town and said she "could name just about every family for blocks around." Despite her widespread acquaintance with other people and the extent to which she and her acquaintances were familiar with each other, her relationships with her family were her major source of enjoyment and comfort. She believed that she and other miners' wives "rely on the family because it's natural. . . . Who do you know better than them? You don't need to guess about what they'll do, or if they'll want to do this or that, or how they'll think if you do.

"When I need emotional support, it's my family I turn to. It isn't always that they help in big things. It's that they want to help in any way . . . and it's the little things that really mean a lot too. Maybe, just someone says, 'Well, we're praying for you' or 'We're right next door,' or 'Just call.' . . . Or they just tap on the door, and they're there, and you know they really care. They help in things where you wouldn't think of asking for help, but it means something to you. . . . If something needs a repair and I can't get my husband to do it, his dad always comes up and does it. I wouldn't ask a friend or a neighbor to do for me, but your family is who you can turn to."

Mary grew up in a mining camp. She explained, "My father and grandfather were miners, my uncles too, and my brothers. It was hard for all of us then. We worked hard. . . . We prayed. We took care of each other. We didn't have much. . . . It was the same for all the families, but we knew to take care of ourselves and others because it *was* hard. If someone needed something and you had it to give, you gave it. . . . That's the way it was, and I wouldn't have given it up for nothing.

"Some had a chance to get away. . . . My husband did. He had the offer to go to Pittsburgh . . . and his uncle went away to Detroit once. I know a few more who tried, but none of them ever stayed for good. . . . They all came back. . . . They're still here right now. After six months my husband came back and so did his uncle. They were just so unhappy. . . . You can't stay away from home. He said he thought about home every day and every night. Nothing was right about living in the city. He said everybody was strangers and nobody was ever real friendly. He didn't like the streets or the houses, nothing. He said he just couldn't take it staying there. No place is like this. It's where your family is, and family is really all you've got. If it's your home, even working in the mines is better than doing something anywhere else."

In addition to family relationships, the women made other important supportive relationships, and nearly always these relationships were with other miners' wives. None of the women had close friendships with women whose husbands were not employed in the mines. The similarities between their own circumstances and those of other miners' wives were central in the formation of close friendships. Such friendships provided an outlet for feelings of frustration, worry, and irritation at the annoyances of daily life that were common to mining.

Nancy believed that strong emotional ties between the women grew out of shared experiences. "We have something in common, like a bond or something. I couldn't talk to L. [an acquaintance], for instance. Her husband is not a miner. She doesn't understand what mining is about. You have to be a miner's wife to understand a miner's wife. You can sympathize with her, because you know what it is about this life makes you feel bad or worried. Someone who doesn't know about what mining is about just knows about miners from what people say about them. . . . When they're on strike, there's not much sympathy. When someone gets hurt, they say, 'Too bad, we're sorry,' but the next day they've forgotten.

"The same things get to be important. . . . Sometimes you don't even have to talk about them. My friend knows what it feels like to worry about if the money'll hold out and what if he gets black lung. . . . And she knows what it's like when my husband's late and you don't know why. . . . She knew what I felt like when my husband got hurt. I didn't have to say anything when T. got his fingers smashed. My friend just came over and sat here. . . . She knew what I was feeling like. My friends are friends because they're miners' wives."

Mary recalled that in the mining camps in the 1930's and 1940's the wives of all the miners were "like one family. Every Sunday morning we'd meet down on the school grounds. All we'd do is talk about how it was yesterday at the mine. We all played cards together, like on nice evenings when they'd get done. . . . And at Bertha [a mining camp] they formed a ball team. The wives would bake things, and after the game everybody got together. It took some of the hardness away for awhile, you know. It was like you could relax and forget about things. When someone got hurt, everybody knew it, and everybody went and helped out. . . . You might bring some food or take the babies home to take care of them. When someone died, everyone pitched in and helped the family. We'd go and clean the house, bring our own curtains and put them up so it'd look nice, make all the food. . . . You wanted to do what you could.

"I think that helped my married life . . . the giving. The friends there helped through the bad times. I felt secure there. I felt I had what I needed, good neighbors. Fifty percent of your good home life was good neighbors. We depended on each other. We'd go and do for someone who needed it. If you had trouble with your kids or needed to talk or needed help somehow . . . you knew it was there. In all the things that was so bad about mining—and it was worse then than now—you had your neighbors. No one wanted to leave when the company told us we had to buy the houses or move. . . . It was more than just the house you had. It was all the other ones that lived in the camp that made it such a home."

The importance of close female friendships also came out in conversations with women who lacked such ties. In particular, the women who lived in isolated rural areas found that making and keeping friendships with other miners' wives was nearly impossible because of the distance between their homes and the homes of other women or between their homes and the closest community. Adding to the problem of distance was the fact that the rural back roads that connected the many small farms and homes in the valleys and on the mountain sides were often so poorly maintained that some women were reluctant to use them except in good weather. The roads that connected mines and larger highways were also often busy with speeding coal trucks that, as Rose said, "drive right in the middle so they won't run off the side. They think nobody has any right to be on the road but them."

Further, the younger rural women tended to have infants or preschool children who left them little time for visiting friends or family. The burdens of child care, homemaking, and for a few, occasionally working outside the home left little time for social interactions with friends. Even the middle-aged and older rural women found their homemaking and outside work often took so much time that they had little free time to spend in making and keeping friends. They felt their lack of friends made them particularly vulnerable to loneliness. Even those who had lived in isolated rural areas for years felt they had never entirely adjusted to being out of contact with other miners' wives.

Cora had lived for many years far back along a twisting country road running into the coal lands. The land adjoined her parents' land, and the house that she and her miner husband purchased had been built by an uncle who had died in a mine accident. Cora and her husband raised two children in the comfortable frame home "back up the holler." In her late middle-age years at the time of our interview, Cora said, "I get pretty lonely back here. I really don't have any close friends. It's too far away.

"I used to talk everything over with my mother and my aunt every day just about. They'd walk over or I'd walk over. They were just up the road. But they're gone now. The house was so old it just got tore down so there's nobody there. It's kind of hard. I really don't talk to any other women much. I guess I try to let my husband and church take care of that [social contacts]. I think the miner's wife, specially if she has children, just has less time for that because she's trying to do so much for her husband. Then if you live way out here like we do, there's no way you're going to see people very often.

"It's hard though. I tried this and that kind of thing. Then I joined the church, and I've been living for the Lord and that helps some. I don't complain much. That's just the way it is . . . but it's hard and it's lonely. I used to pray that other families would move up here. Before we tore the old house down, I used to think about having a neighbor, but who'd want to buy it and fix it up when even we didn't? . . . I just had to get used to being alone. That's what I told myself after my mother went. 'You just gotta get used to it.'"

Sharon, a younger woman with two small children, agreed that not having friends close was hard. "I really don't have any friends. . . . I really don't talk to anybody a great deal of the time. We just live too far out here. I talk to my husband but it's not the same as a girlfriend. . . . He's got his problems, and I think he don't understand mine. He wants to but he's got things on his mind . . . work and all . . . and unless we're sick, I think he thinks I've got it pretty good and what more do I want. I've got a car now, but the friends I used to have aren't close. . . . It's a whole afternoon if I go to see them and take the children . . . and it's a lot of work to do that too, so I stay home a lot. You know, with two children, you just . . . well, me and my anxieties just stay home alone."

Paula, another younger woman, said, "Well, loneliness now, that's been a problem. Both my parents are dead, and I don't have any other family besides my younger brother, and I can't really talk to him a whole lot. We're close, but it's not the same because he's not a woman and he's young. My husband's family is here, but there are times when I want to talk to someone that's mine. He don't understand that, and I don't really know how to say what it is—just that sometimes I wish there was someone here that was *mine*. His friends are here and they're my friends too. But one thing with us having kids, most of his friends don't have kids and they work, so a lot of the time I'm home in the day by myself. . . . That's when it really hits you, and I really don't have anyone to talk to. Sometimes there's just so much on my mind. Yesterday, I just started to cry. It gets so bad, and I just don't have anybody to talk to."

The women told me that in the rural and coal-mining areas of West Virginia, youthful marriages remained the norm. A few believed that marrying young was a coal-mining tradition, a belief that is well supported by researchers who have written about West Virginia, Kentucky, and southern Ohio families (Brooks 1973; Coles 1971; Maggard 1990b; Scott 1988). The older women (now in their mid-forties and older) had married at fifteen or sixteen and most of the younger women had married at eighteen or nineteen. Only two had married later, both at twenty-two. The men they married were also young: at most their husbands were only a year or two older. It was not just they that had married young, they said; everyone they knew had married young.

Beth, now in her late fifties, had married at fifteen. She explained, "My mother married young. My grandmother married young. . . . Everybody did, and we had a wonderful family. If there was a woman didn't marry young, then people asked why unless she was taking care of younger ones or maybe teaching school. It seemed right, and I guess that's where it comes from. When everybody you know growing up is getting married and getting a home of their own, then that's what you want to do. We never asked if we was too young once you got to fifteen or sixteen. . . . I even knew girls who got married younger even though that *was* too young. You didn't think about things like that then. You met someone and you got married. And you married a miner. My dad and grandad were miners, and I was proud to be a coal miner's wife . . . always was."

Marrying a miner was, she explained, "natural because if you're raised in a mining family, who else did you meet . . . go and associate with? You didn't associate with the college crowd because you didn't go to college. You didn't associate with any well-to-do because, here you are, you're from Scotts Run, Bertha Hill, mining camps all! You're working in the A & P or

cleaning houses, and you didn't associate with them. You'd
know the preacher or the teachers, but usually they were
married. Mostly, all you knew were coal miners. You knew
everybody in the camp. You knew which boys were rough or
drank too much. . . . You got to know boys from other camps
and some from town, but all miners. It just seemed natural."

Several younger women recalled that their parents, particularly their mothers, had not wished their daughters to marry
until they had finished high school. As an adolescent, Paula
had acceded to her mother's wishes and entered college. She
left the university in her second year to marry the young miner
she had been seeing. "My mother wanted me to graduate from
college. Didn't want me to get married until I graduated and
worked for a while .˙. . and never to a coal miner . . . but I
wanted to. Of course, I'd always lived with it. I mean, most of
the boys I went to school with were going to go into the mines,
and most girls got married right away. So I went to college and
ended up marrying a miner anyway. But that's who you meet
being from down here. . . . And why wait if you want to get
married? . . . It didn't make any sense to me to wait for two
more years just to get married. We loved each other. We wanted
to start our home, so why wait?"

For the middle-aged and older women, marrying young had
also meant dropping out of school. At the time of their
marriages, both girls and boys in mining families in the Appalachian coal areas commonly left school in the eighth, ninth, or
tenth grades to work and contribute to the family's income, to
care for younger brothers and sisters still at home, or to marry
and begin their own families. Few, even among the early
middle-aged women, had expected to earn a high-school diploma. One of the older women, like some other women in
Appalachian mining areas, had completed high school by obtaining an equivalency (Maggard 1990b; Scott 1988).

Social and economic change in the decades that separated
the older and younger women had changed the ages at which
young people left school, and all but one of the younger
women had completed high school. Other differences between
the younger and older women in regard to education were

evident. It was the young women, not the older women, who considered the value of learning from textbooks and classroom instructors debatable. Their concerns were largely pragmatic. They saw broad formal education as a means of expanding one's awareness of the world and oneself, but it was the realities of life that had to be dealt with day to day. A practical education, even the limited one formerly provided by the settlement schools (Knipe and Lewis 1971; Painter 1987), was what was needed to survive. In the younger women's opinions, even in contemporary times the most useful knowledge was gained by living, working, and meeting the crises of life.

Sharon commented, "There's a certain amount you need to learn from school. . . . You have to learn to read and write and know how to work out your income and expenses so you have enough to get by. You need to learn about the government too, and you understand things better if you learn some about history and other things. But the things you have to learn about living, you have to learn from doing the best you can. You can't learn from books how to deal with what you're going to run into. . . . No one can tell you how to deal with all the problems you're going to have. . . . No one can teach you what it's going to be like, because no one's life is going to be exactly like yours. . . . You just have to do it, and then you learn.

"You deal with the problems you have. You deal with your own morals, your own values. You deal with it all. You piece it all together. You read about other people's problems. You talk to other people. . . . You try different things. You learn to think for yourself. That never ends, and no one can teach you that. School may help some [people] . . . maybe in the city or if a person is going to go on [continue their education]. But, well, here the economy is geared to mining. There's nothing else here. The boys just slough through high school saying, 'I don't need this. I'm going to make $50.00 a day in the mines.' And girls are going to marry miners—that's who you get to know around here. The boys are going in the mines, and the girls are going to be homemakers. School can't teach any of them how it really is. They have to learn by doing it."

The older women's opinions about the value of education differed somewhat. They were equally confident about the necessity and the value of learning through living, but they placed a higher value on formal education than the younger women did. The most important potential benefit of education was a better job, a job not associated with mining. There were other meanings associated with education, however, and one of them was its effects on a person's self-esteem. Beth recalled, "I didn't get to go to high school. I couldn't buy books, and I was ashamed because I didn't have clothes like the other children had. Everyone said then you didn't need much past reading, writing, and figuring, and I knew that if I wanted things, . . . really wanted things, I would have to get a job, so I got a job. I needed that job, and it made things easier for my family. And, you know, you expected to do what you could do as soon as you were old enough.

"But I felt bad because I couldn't go to school. I just can't describe what kind of a feeling it was to watch other people walking to school, and there I was walking to work. They were reading books, and I wasn't going to get to read them. . . . There were so many things I could see I wasn't going to get to do, because I had to work. No more school for me, and I could see that people who finished school were getting better jobs. So when I got married, I felt like my children had to go to school whether they wanted to or not. They didn't want to, but I kept saying, 'Go another year. That's all I'm asking is go one more year. So after, they was so into it, they got on sports, they got on things they really enjoyed and all that, and they stopped thinking about quitting. Now they have good jobs, every one of them. They'll never be in the mines. And I'm not saying I'd change one thing in my life. I wouldn't. But when they was little, I thought if school kept them out of the mines, then they were going to go to school."

Most of the women's husbands had even fewer years of education than their wives. About a third of the eighteen men had completed high school, all of them among the younger men. None of the men who were older than their middle thirties had

completed high school, and some of the older men had gone no
further than the fourth or fifth grades before leaving school to
work in the mines. Their financial contribution to their families had been considered more essential than education; and, as
Mary said of her husband, "It wasn't like it is now. It was
school or food on the table, and what choice was there? He was
eleven, almost twelve. He was old enough, he was big enough,
and there was ten in his family. He stayed in school until his
dad got hurt. But when his dad got hurt, he went to work . . .
and he would've soon anyway. He says now he would have
liked to have had more schooling, but work puts food on the
table, and what else could he do?"

Mary's husband himself recalled, "I never thought much
about it, not about going all the way and finishing school,
anyway. I don't think I even knew anyone that did, not
then anyway—maybe some, the preacher's kids or if your dad
worked in the store—but most young boys went into the
mines. I went in right where my dad had got hurt, the same
place. I had his tools at first and his lamp and all. I was scared
at first too. There's strange noises like you never heard before
in a mine, but I looked forward to it, to earning money. I was
just a little guy, but I was putting food on the table, and it made
me feel good. . . . I wasn't grown up, but I worked like a man,
and I had a man's responsibilities. I didn't miss school. . . . We
didn't know anything else."

Many of the women worked outside their homes when they
were first married, but the arrival of the first child meant
leaving outside employment to become full-time homemakers.
Few thought of themselves as having postponed careers for, as
Beth said, "men bring the check home and women make the
home." Homemaking responsibilities were central in the lives
of even the several women who had thoughts of more education or training for self-employment. With few exceptions,
wives found employment outside the home only when financial conditions made it imperative.

When a woman had to work outside the home or, as in a few
cases, strongly desired to do so, she carried out her full- or part-
time job in addition to usual homemaking routines. She

expanded daily routines by rising earlier to begin household or child care chores. Children were taken to relatives or neighbors to be cared for or, in the case of the older women, to a settlement house. After, as Nancy said, "already working for a couple of hours, then I went on to work to do eight more." The pattern was repeated after work, and the women came home to prepare dinner and complete household and child care.

Mary believed that women's lives were more stressful than men's lives despite the fact that the miners' wives did not face the dangers of the mines. "There's not a minute where you can't find some work that needs to be done. I was a big girl and strong, and I could work all day and go work some more at night. But it was hard, and I remember being so tired at night. I used to get up in the morning, take care of his clothes and lunch bucket, take care of the babies, get them all dressed, and walk down the hill and all the way to the settlement house carrying the littlest one. Then I'd walk on into town and go to work, and then, in the evening, I go in reverse and end up walking up the hill to home again."

For the most part, wives did not ask husbands to help with housework or child care nor did they expect them to take over some part of these chores. Even when the husbands were on strike or laid off, they were likely to spend the hours that were free of work in masculine activities such as taking care of cars, doing minor carpentry chores around the house, watching television, reading, or meeting with friends. A few of the younger women had different expectations for their husbands and said they had made it clear that when they needed to work outside the house, their husbands had to help in household chores.

When it was necessary to work outside the home, the local economic situation in combination with the women's lack of marketable skills and education meant that the work they found was often low paying and physically tiring. Most of the available jobs, even in good economic times, were low-paying clerical, service, or laboring jobs. In poor economic times, many of those jobs disappeared, and homemakers would look for any type of "honest" work they could find. Like many women in mining families in the Appalachian areas (Maggard,

1988), the women said they had done "just about everything—cleaned houses, waited tables, worked in the hospital, babysat, just anything that I could find to do that would pay something, anything."

Rose recalled that her oldest daughter expressed surprise when her mother said she knew how to drive a farm tractor. "I told her there was one year when we wouldn't have had anything to eat if I hadn't got a job working on a farm. He [the farmer] didn't want to hire me because he didn't think I could do it. But I talked to the preacher, and he went over and said, 'Yes, she can,' and I learned it all. I even helped at slaughtering. . . . That was the hardest thing I had to do. But I could do everything else, and I did."

Despite the fact that taking on a full- or part-time job meant obtaining what was often badly needed additional income, many of the women felt inner conflict when homemaking competed with wage earning. Cora's children were grown, but in the past she had worked outside the home during strikes and layoffs so the family could buy food and pay their bills. She said, "You know, I had to help out, and I was glad I could. But I'm sorry too because when you're working, you miss a lot of things. I couldn't go anywhere. Everything had to be done at home after work. There'd be times when we'd all want to go somewhere, and I'd have to tell them to go and go ahead without me. . . . I wanted to go, but there'd be all these things that had to be done at home. Then, I'd feel bad when they'd go. And if they didn't go, then I'd feel bad that they didn't get to go. We needed the money. There was no way we could have paid our bills if I hadn't worked. It really helped out. But I missed a lot, and they missed out on some things. . . . And they needed me at home, too."

A younger woman, Nancy, recalled, "I had to work and I felt I should work, but when Mary [her daughter] was small, I'd get guilty feelings about spending more time with her. Even now, when I see someone who's three years old or two years old, I try . . . I really try . . . and I can't remember her at that age. That really bothers me now. And when I was working, I felt that I should have been more responsible to her and try to be home with her more. And when I was at home, there was just so much to have to do. I don't know if it ever made any difference, and maybe it never did, but I wish I would have been with her more."

Often husbands reacted negatively to their wives' outside employment even when the mines were on strike or the men laid off from work. When tensions arose at home as the result of the women's outside employment, women experienced additional distress. Nancy had worked occasionally from the earliest days of her marriage, and she said her husband's reaction to her working had created conflict between them even though she had worked out of necessity. Her absence from home caused tensions that eventually led the family into ongoing arguments.

"Just about every day my husband would say, 'I wish you weren't working. I'll be glad when you quit.' He'd say it so much, I'd get out of sorts. I wasn't working exactly because I wanted to, but he never really accepted it. Then we'd just go back and forth and back and forth, and then we just had to drop it. It's not like he blamed me for working. He knew I had to work, but he never liked it. I think I took some of the bad feeling he had about the company, but that made me upset too. I wasn't the one who said 'walk out,' but I had to help earn the extra money to get by on.

"Then when he finally was back at work, we missed each other; we'd hardly see each other. We'd still need the money, and I'd keep on for a while; but he'd be going to work when I got home, and I'd be going to work when he got home, and it would get bad for us not to have any time together. It was always that way. . . . It started with him being bothered because I wasn't home, and then it just went on until finally I'd quit. It'd get to the point where I didn't want to go to work, and I didn't want to come home. There were a couple of times when I didn't want to quit. I liked what I was doing, and I wanted to keep on. But you know it was just too much at home. . . . We'd just be at each other too much."

Some of the middle-aged and older women, although they agreed that being at home was best when children were young, took a different view of working outside the home at other times. They looked back on the sacrifices they had made over the years and felt that, in their middle and older years, finding desirable and enjoyable outside work helped compensate for past sacrifices. After years of serving their families, it was their turn to "do their thing." Working outside the home at work that they enjoyed brought relief from the restrictiveness of full-time homemaking and also helped them expand their social networks.

Rose worked because she wanted to work. She said that when her youngest child was in the last year of high school, "I told my husband that I spent thirty some years cleaning and cooking and raising the kids, and now he's going to have to put up with a little dust because . . . now I found something I really want to do. I used to worry about my work getting done, where now I see there's something else. Before, the kids and him were always the most important thing, and I stayed home and done my work except when we just had to have the money. But I've changed in that the housework will be here when I'm gone, and I want to do what I want to do now. . . . I want to do something I really enjoy."

Carol, whose youngest child was entering high school, said, "All my kids are in school now, and we had an agreement that when all the kids were in school then I'd go out and get a job I want. It helped a lot. . . . It gives you a chance to get involved with something where . . . Like, well now, I'm more able and willing to discuss things, more open about things. I used to be more shy before—kept things in. Now that I'm working, it's different. I'm more social and he is too. He didn't like it at first. But now he gets into listening to what I'm doing, and he even does more around the house. I think it's hard to explain but working has gotten to be something that does us both good."

Mary summed up the opinions of many of the other older women when she talked about her years of working outside the home. "I done everything. I always worked when we had a need. I never complained. Now I work at what I like. And if things are just not perfect at home, then they're not. That's all. I tell you, the husbands like to have you at home, but they wouldn't like it if you told them they couldn't do what they wanted to do. Now I have just got to the point where I am going to do the things I like to do. My daughter said, 'Mom, you deserve it,' and she's right."

Like homemakers everywhere, the miners' wives organized their daily lives around the demands of husband, family, work, and their own needs. Unlike most homemakers, however, all but two of the women had husbands who were working, and had always worked, on shifts that systematically moved around the days and nights. The men who worked from early morning to midafternoon changed after three weeks to a mid-afternoon to late-night shift. Three weeks later the same men changed again to a late-night to early-morning shift. Three weeks later they would again work from early morning to mid-afternoon.

Shift work had always been onerous and stifling to their social and emotional lives, but before children came along the women and their husbands felt the situation was manageable. They compromised on shared activities, selectively let go of some activities, and cultivated social relationships with other young couples on similar shift schedules. But when children came along, the increased work load involved in caring for an infant, maintaining the home, and sometimes working outside the house created new difficulties for families. In nearly every family, attempting to work around the miner's irregular working hours brought intense frustrations and conflicts.

Sharon said, "It gets to the point where I don't know how to handle it. This whole shift business bears around my whole life because I can't really go out and leave the baby here. He's asleep. I can't invite anyone to come to my house. He's asleep. I can't plan for us to go anywhere together . . . even to church on Sunday or just to go shopping, except for every couple months. Before the baby was born, I just went, but I can't do that now. And my friends have babies too, so I can't have them here when he's asleep. Well . . . they understand because their husbands do that too, but still this doesn't make no consolation to me."

Most of the women had experimented with various ways of adjusting the family schedule to the miners' hours, and trying out various solutions had led eventually to routines that were minimally acceptable although they seldom eliminated the major problems. A few families learned to cope with the constantly changing working hours by scheduling daily activities as if the family activities were separable from the working man's hours. That is, the family activities included his participation when such participation was compatible with his working schedule and excluded him when it was not.

Most of the women felt such solutions were not acceptable because their husbands would too often have missed being a part of the family's activities. Both the family and the miner would have been deprived of each other's company. Rose and Paula were among the women who had tried this method in order to facilitate or participate in their children's planned activities. Unless their husbands were willing to cut short their sleeping hours, the children's schedules were incompatible with two of the three working shifts. When the two women compared their experiences with this method of coping with rotating shifts, they found it had had only temporary benefits.

"It seemed to work for a while, but then it got so the girls [their daughters] had all these things that their dad was never a part of, and more and more we just were like living different lives. We'd shop without him except when he was on night shift. We'd go to church without him. We'd go to the grandparents' without him. We'd go to all of the school things without him. Go to the games without him. We'd be talking about something that happened, and he wouldn't know anything about it. He'd get upset, and then the girls got upset, and they didn't want to do things without him. He said he just felt left out all the time, and he didn't like it and neither did we."

A more frequently used solution was to try and organize the family schedules around the miners' hours. Ginny said, "I tried everything, and there just isn't any real good way to work around his shifts. The best thing is that once in awhile you got him on a normal schedule like the rest of the world. But that's only once every couple months, and the rest of the time you're working on different hours than the rest of the world. It's just a constant thing that you got to deal with. You got to change the hours you sleep, change the hours you spend together, change everything when he changes hours."

The difficulties accompanying the attempted solutions were a persistent source of problems and frustrations for all members of the family (Althouse 1974; Portner 1983). Communication between wives and husbands, social activities, and relationships with children were all adversely affected when the family tried to accommodate its schedule to changing shifts or to maintain a normal schedule despite the shift being worked. When the family members adjusted their schedule to the miner's schedule, the family routines were often at odds with those of schools, stores, and churches. When the family maintained a different daily schedule from the miner, it was difficult to find mutually suitable times for sharing a day's experiences, solving problems, meeting with friends, or spending time with children.

Louise complained, "Shift work is really irritating. Nothing about it is right. Nothing ever works best for us together. The day shift is the best shift for me because he's more on regular working hours. But he doesn't particularly enjoy it because he hates getting up so early and feels like he's more tired on day shift. He likes the afternoon shift. But I hate it because it makes for a long, long, lonely evening for me and the kids, and in the summertime it would be so nice to be able to be out and doing what other families are doing. For him to be working then, well, it creates a hardship because we don't get enough time together. Midnight shift is difficult for him and me because he can't get enough sleep here at home during the day, and I mind having to tiptoe around or not do my work until late. I just don't like changing shifts at all. . . . It's just a constant irritating thing. . . . I never really get used to it."

Nearly all of the women believed that shift work added difficulties and dangers to their husbands' work. They worried about the strains their husbands experienced in adjusting to new shifts and about the increased chances of injuries when the men were tired. Karen said, "It's a problem that's common. . . . He's irritable on the night shift. He says he's tired a lot because he can't sleep in the day for a couple of weeks and then, just when he does, the shift changes. It takes him a week to get used to being on another shift. But night shift is the worst for me, because on night shifts I worry more about him because maybe he'll get only three or four hours' sleep in the day and it's much more dangerous when they're tired. . . . They can get careless . . . not pay attention like they should."

The women's concerns about the increased danger caused by shift work were intensified by their husbands' recounting of other workers' accidents and injuries due to tiredness and, for some women, by their own husbands' injuries. Ginny recalled, "He tries to say it's not a big thing. But he tells me when this one or that one gets hurt, and a lot of times it's when they go in on the first day or maybe two three days after changing. There's always more accidents when shifts change. And more will be off [called in sick], and then he's gonna have to do someone else's work, and that's more dangerous too. When he was hurt, he wasn't getting enough sleep and not paying enough attention to what he did. . . . He says it was his fault because he was tired. He just changed shifts, and he can't sleep right at first. He was lucky, only hurt, but others aren't always that lucky."

For some women, the problems caused over time by their husbands' rotating shifts combined to become the basis of long-term strains and disagreements. Some problems had become so difficult to resolve and so likely to cause conflict between wives and husbands that they no longer discussed them. However, coping with the problem in this way had also led to the accumulation of underlying tensions that then had become attached to other problems. Laura, for example, complained, "We can't talk about it. . . . We've done that and done that until we just stopped. . . . We just get mad at each other. My feelings about it just sit there and don't get out. He knows there's not so many things I'm dissatisfied with but this changing shifts. But we can't talk about it. It gets us both mad. It's all the things like whenever we need him, he's on the night shift. And he's cranky, he's tired, he don't want to be bothered with any problems at home, and he never wants to do anything. Sometimes it's like a real thing there between us. I hate to think we're going to go through the rest of our lives three weeks days, three weeks afternoons, three weeks nights."

The family problems that accompanied the miners' rotating shift work were some of the most persistent and troublesome problems for workers involved in mining. Friends and relatives worked on similar schedules, and the women knew that disruptions in family routines as a result of shift work were common among other couples. They perceived shift work as one of the most distressing aspects of their husbands' jobs, and they were aware of the effects of their frustrations and resentments on family relationships. Yet they saw shift work, like the dangers of mining, as an inevitable and nearly unchangeable aspect of mining that had to be accepted.

In our conversations, it became clear that most of the women believed that God's will would be the final determiner of the outcomes of their lives and of their families' lives. They did not discount skill, experience, wisdom, caution, careful planning, and even luck as casual factors but, believed that over and above these considerations, the fate that God decreed for each person would prevail. Beth explained, "He has a plan for everybody. . . . That's the way it is even if you think it's not. God has a plan for everybody. He controls everything. They say sometimes accidents could have been prevented, but you never know when He's decided it's your time. You might work all your life in the mines and not get hurt, and then one day you go to work, and there's an accident. It's God's will for you."

Yet, in a half-skeptical, half-amused but half-believing manner, many of the women felt that certain routines for helping their husbands prepare for work, putting certain things in his lunch bucket, or having certain thoughts while he was at work would help to ensure his safety. They found that the routines, the articles in the lunch bucket, or the particular thoughts associated with uneventful, stress-free working days in the mines helped them feel they had done at least some small thing to increase his safety. They laughed at their own accounts of these superstitious habits, and yet the strength of these security measures was evidenced by the care they took to follow such routines and their feelings of uneasiness if they neglected a routine.

Cora had been packing a lunch bucket for her husband for "more years than I can count, and I put everything in his lunch bucket in the same way every day. And there are some things he likes to have every day. And if I don't have them, well, I don't like not to have what he wants in there. If I don't, I worry some. It's not a major worry, but I'll think about it all day. . . . He's more on my mind if I forget or if I leave something out. Maybe it don't matter but it makes me feel easier."

Another woman described the way in which she laid out her husband's work clothes with each article in the same place and always in the same order. A few of the women said they always made sure their husbands had pictures of their children with them, and one younger woman always tucked a note to her husband under his sandwiches. Everyone recognized these routines as superstitious, and yet they valued them because it eased their worry. As Mary and several others said, "There ain't no job like mining, no job where you don't know when he leaves in the morning, if he'll be back. . . . Anything you can do to make it better makes you feel better."

Believing in the will of God and relying on superstitious routines to ease their worries about their husbands provided a small measure of temporary relief from the knowledge that many of the dangers in the mine were unpredictable and uncontrollable. But some women said that such measures were less helpful than a deliberate and conscious refusal to recognize the high probability of accidents and injuries. They believed their own active denial helped reduce their worries because it was a barrier against the recognition and visualization of death by crushing, suffocation, or burning. Carol said, "I can't think about what he does. If I do, I just sit down and bawl. . . . I can't do it. I really try not to think about it. I try just to keep my mind on other things. I don't want to think about it. I don't want to hear about it. I don't want to know about it. . . ."

Nancy felt the same way: "I don't think about what he does. I know because he tells me, but I don't think about it. This really hits me hard. . . . My father was a miner. My brothers are miners. Some I know well have died down there, and I know about what happens. If you don't know, then maybe it doesn't get you like it gets me. It scares me, it upsets me, and I can't think about it. I don't really want to hear about it, and that's hard because he wants to talk and I don't want to hear."

However, rejecting thoughts about the dangers that threatened their husbands did not allow a complete escape from exposure to conversations about mining. The processes of mining, accidents, threats of accidents, injuries, close calls, and the other experiences of mining were the primary subjects of conversation among the couples' social groups. As Ginny explained, "Our friends are miners—that's what they talk about. It upsets me to hear it, but that's what they want to talk about. Everybody talks about their work because that's what you do. . . . Miners are just the same . . . but when they get into talking about what almost happened to someone or how the other one got hurt today, I have to leave the room."

Most of the women readily admitted that although rejection of thoughts about the dangers of mining brought temporary relief, the threats to their husbands' lives were central components of the conditions of their lives, and the fear they felt was not in the long run reduced by denial. Nevertheless, all but a few felt they regarded this aspect of their lives in a relatively pragmatic way. Nearly all said they had known the hazards of mining before they married. Most of them believed that as children they had observed and shared in the worries and anxieties of their mothers. All but a few felt that, by the time they married, they were well aware of the stresses to be faced as a miner's wife.

As adults, they were determined to deal with the events of their lives in practical ways. If shift work separated a husband from the family, the family would adjust its schedule to his. If additional income was needed, they would work outside the home. If bearing more than their share of child care and home maintenance would relieve their husbands of work and worry, they would carry a greater load. They would do what must be done to nurture children and husbands and maintain their homes.

Yet their willingness to accept these conditions was not without self-criticism. Some of the women said they occasionally reflected on the place of women in their society and the long-term effects of their attitudes on their mental health. They were clearly aware that, like their forebears, they had the ability to do what must be done, but, perhaps unlike their forbears, they questioned the personal costs. Moreover, carrying out the responsibilities of the traditional miner's wife made some women develop a new feeling of self-awareness. If they could move into the wage earner role when necessary, why not when desirable? If they could support and sometimes motivate their husbands during conflicts with the coal companies, why not become activists for their own interests?

Rose, for example, confided, "I think that I used to try to be everything for my husband because I thought that made it better for him and better for me too. . . . After you get a little older, you got a little more sense. You get to know more about the world, and you get to see what you can do . . . what makes you feel like life's worth something and what makes you miserable. Coal mining is the worst kind of job, but you can't just leave, and you don't want to. . . . You married this man because you loved him, and you wanted to marry him. But you start thinking about who you are too.

"Then you find out you got to think ahead . . . think of what happens to you after a while, plan ahead. You got to learn to do this no matter how it hurts. . . . You got two or three little children, and you got to think about them . . . about the future. If something happens to your husband, you're all your children have. What would you do then if you'd spent all your time on your husband? If you don't think of yourself, think of your health, of what you can do, then who will take care of your children? It's just the hardest thing to do because you've got too much on you already, but you just have to think of yourself too."

Despite their knowledge of the conditions of life for mining families and their pragmatic view of their own lives, the women's emotional ties to the men who went under the mountains to work each day bound them into a life context that sometimes seemed overwhelming. They knew the history of the mines, the work of mining, the attitudes of the mining companies, and mining politics. They felt little optimism that anything would change. Second only to the men who actually worked day by day in the mines, the miners' wives lived the conditions of life the mining industry created.

THREE

Unseen Dangers: The Perils of Mining

Tales of death and heroism, injuries, near injuries, and narrow escapes are themes that have been woven through the lives of generations of West Virginia miners. Among nonmining families, such tales were folklore, yesterday's and today's news, events that happened to someone else. To mining families, the tales were alive, close, and painful examples of the consequences of working under the ground. They told of what could, had, or might happen today or tomorrow to a neighbor or friend or the person with whom you shared dinner, conversation, life.

Talking about mining was a part of the everyday routine of many miners' wives. Their husbands, like working men and women everywhere, talked about their work when they came home. But mining talk contained an element not often present in the daily work conversation of other people. Miners talked about the unpredictable and ever present dangers of mining as well as about their coworkers, supervisors, and daily tasks.

Mining has always been a highly dangerous occupation with a death and injury rate matched by few other occupations, perhaps by none (Scott 1988). In the years between 1897 and 1939 (the years in which the oldest of the eighteen women were growing up), millions of tons of coal came rumbling out of the mines in West Virginia (State of West Virginia 1986) at the cost of thousands of miners' lives. During that period, 346 men died in the West Virginia mines each year. Nearly every day a mining family lost a member to the mines, and dozens of men suffered injuries.

In the next forty-one years, when most of the rest of the women in the book were growing up, going through school, getting married, and beginning their families, coal productivity rose and fell in response to the changing demands of the economy and, with the advent of mining machinery, the number of people engaged in mining decreased. Safety procedures, as well as mining methods, also changed during these years. The total number of deaths and of serious injuries in the mines began to show significant reductions. Nevertheless, from 1939 to 1980 injuries were still commonplace, and 146 men died each year. In other words, somewhere in the state of West Virginia during every one of those forty-one years, a mining family lost a member every two and a half days.

As coal markets continued to fluctuate, and mechanized mining began to maintain adequate productivity with fewer workers, death and injury rates in the mines continued to decline. In the five years between 1981 and 1986, production of coal was low, and only slightly more than thirty-two thousand people worked for the coal companies in the state of West Virginia. Yet even in those five years, an average of 22.6 died in the mines each year. One miner was lost from a mining family about every other week (State of West Virginia 1988).

Despite the decline in deaths and injuries in the mines, mining remained work in which death occurred frequently, unexpectedly, and often without relation to the worker's skill, caution, and safety measures. Further, the actual hazards of mining—that is, the risk of cave-ins, explosions, toxic gasses, and other dangers—could combine with human error to create situations in which any forewarning of an accident was unlikely. The hazards, the actual conditions in which the miners worked, and the unpredictable and seemingly random nature of mining accidents were all a part of the miners' talk; the stories the miners told of close calls were hallmarks of the occupation.

The miners' families' fears and anxieties about the dangers of mining were not unrealistic or exaggerated by the "second hand" nature of their information. The coal seams ran hundreds of feet below the mountaintops, and the thousands of tons of rock, soil, and water that lay over the heads of the miners far below had never rested easily. Knowledge of this was a part of the fear of "underground" that kept many men from becoming miners. Even without any education in geology, the miners knew that the layers of rock that composed the mountains were pinned down tightly by the immense pressure of their weight. But, as the coal beneath was removed, the layers of rock might shift. These shifts, in turn, might split other layers of rock and bring new pressure to bear on those strata that formed the tunnel roofs below.

Such pressure shifts could cause pieces or avalanches of rock to fall into the mine sections. Other pressures might move inward against the tunnel walls forcing them to shift and rupture, spilling fractured rock into the miners' working spaces. The ground could heave up beneath the tunnel and release an underground spring or a pocket of trapped gas; or water draining from the mountain above could completely fill the mine spaces and trap the miners. Even the machinery of mining presented dangers. It was complex, heavy, dangerous to use, prone to break down, and in need of almost constant attention. Further, space was cramped, illumination was minimal, and there was a constant pall of dust.

At the "face," the foremost part of the mining tunnel, the mining machinery (the continuous miner) bit into the coal seam with parallel sets of heavy, rotating drill bits taller than a man. The walls and roof of the tunnel were cut only high enough and wide enough to accommodate the machine, with very little free space at each side for the men who served it. A wrong movement, a fall, or stumble, or a miscalculated step would put the miner in what might be fatal or injurious contact with the machine.

The roof above the machinery was supported by timbers and by steel bolts driven up into the layers of rock. The roof and the walls of the tunnels might or might not be stable. The layers of rock pinned by the bolts might not be dense enough to hold the bolts, or the side walls might not be sturdy enough to withstand the sideways pressures. Rotten rock in the roof or sides could hold for a while and then break and move, falling down or pushing out the side walls. The weight of the mountain above might shift as the coal seams were chewed into, and all or part of the roof or sides might fall.

As the coal was torn from the seam, dust filled the air. If methane gas was trapped within the coal seam, it might be released along with the dust. The combination of dust and gas was a constant threat in the presence of the high-voltage electrical cables used to run the mining machine and conveyor belts. The dangerous mixture of dust and gas had to be constantly expelled from the mine to prevent its igniting explosively and blasting through the mine like a traveling bomb (Althouse 1974; Arble 1976; Witt and Dotter 1979). Poor ventilation, even for a short period of time, or motors and fans that stopped working presented an immediate danger to the miners.

In some mines vaults of gas had accumulated in unventilated, old, or forgotten shafts and tunnels. Maps prepared by the engineers showed the locations of many of these old mine workings, but no one knew how many were not shown. Every miner did know, however, that hundreds of old mine workings were likely never to have been mapped. An abandoned, partially worked coal seam might lie behind any face or beyond any of the walls being chewed out by the continuous miner. When an old seam was broken into, it would release its built-up store of deadly gas and claim the lives of the men working at the face. No one would know of its presence until someone died.

There was danger from water as well. The water that seeped down from the mountain above or up from underground springs might cause the discomfort of working with wet and cold feet and legs, but the risk of electrocution was a greater danger. The miners who maintained the mining machine might have to stand or kneel in water while they repaired electrical connections or wired new connections to extend wiring farther into the mine. Pumps drained out the seeping water, and they too had to be kept in repair by men who might have to stand or kneel in water. In some mines, if the pumps failed for very long, men would be trapped in their working sections by water that filled the lower portions of the tunnels.

In addition to being exposed to the dangers created by machinery, cave-ins, gas, and water, the miners usually had to work in cramped confines with very little light and a great deal of dust and noise. There was very little working space in a mine because cutting and hauling out rock cost money. Consequently tunnels were no wider or higher than was necessary to remove the coal, and working conditions were so cramped that heavy work was particularly tiring. Miners entered some mines while lying down on a carrier called a "mantrip" that would carry them to the working sections. Once there, they might have to work stooped over, kneeling, or in a squatting position (Althouse 1974; Scott 1988; Witt and Dotter 1979).

There was no natural light in a coal mine and little manmade light except where light was crucial. The miner's headlamp was often the only illumination, and even this poor illumination was diminished by the dust that hung in the air. Despite the constant pull of powerful ventilation fans, the dust filtered through the miners' clothing, coated their skin, worked its way down through their hair, and lined their nostrils. Every intake of breath deposited microscopic, sharp-edged particles onto the sensitive membranes in their lungs.

The mining process was also noisy, and noise in itself was a hazard for the miners because the sounds of machinery could hide the sounds of danger. The ear-numbing sound of the huge drilling bits on the continuous miner as they chewed into the solid rock face mingled with the thump and rattle of coal being dumped behind the bits. The conveyors that carried the coal away added their constant noise to the general cacophony that filled and bounced around the rock-walled, small spaces. When the sounds of mining filled the air, any small sound that indicated danger, like the snap of a bad electrical connection or the warning words of another miner, could not be heard.

When new miners began their work, they had to learn the hazards common in the mines and the specific hazards connected with their own tasks. They learned the conditions, cues, and signs that indicated potential danger and about situations that increased the likelihood of accidents. They found out, for example, that working with a new miner was more hazardous than working with another experienced miner. Working at another miner's job, working overtime, or changing work shifts was conducive to accidents, injuries, and fatalities, they learned.

Moreover, the new miners discovered that a poorly maintained machine, overlooked safety procedures, pressure to produce more coal, and tiredness or inexperience could be the deadliest of combinations (Althouse 1974; Corbin 1981; Scott 1988).

As the miners learned about their work, they shared much of what they learned with their families. Consequently the miners' wives and children learned what their husbands and fathers must know and do, even though the women and children might never have been in a working mine. Women in second and third generation mining families grew up learning about mining. Every day as children, they heard their families speak of the work of mining and tell of events from their parents' or grandparents' childhood. They knew about the close calls and near misses, the scraped knuckles and bruised limbs, and the sprained backs. They watched the men come out of the mines day by day dirty and exhausted. Sometimes they saw them walk out with injuries, or be carried out dead, or not return at all.

Mary explained, "When you're raised in a mining family, you knew what it was like. I knew the things that my father did and my brothers, knew how hard it was. My mother had a boarding house with seven boarders that went into the mine. They become family too. They'd all talk about mining and that's how I knew. I grew up with this sort of thing. I knew what they had to do, and I knew how they had to do it, how hard it was. And I knew the fear of underground.

"You heard about it all . . . the gas, the roof falls, the ones that got hurt, the ones that saved somebody. You always heard about it at dinner and in the evenings. You heard which sections were bad, the ones no one ever wanted to work. You heard about which one [mine company] was the worst of all to work for, and how they treated you. We knew everything the company did.

"We all talked about things that we was worried about, and we all saw the things that happened. I saw my father go in, seen him come out injured. Seen my brother go in, and seen him brought out dead. Seen my other brother ruin his lungs. Seen some come out burned, crushed, blood all over. Nothing, no way, can ever compare to being a coal miner. You never get

used to it . . . to having somebody that's yours down there. . . .
It's a feeling that you just can't express. You feel that every day
something is going to be took away from you."

Beth, reflecting about how she learned about mining and
what life is like for mining families, compared her life with her
mother's. She felt she had been luckier than her mother. Her
mother's life was much harder; the mines were "not working
good for years and there was a lot of us" to feed and clothe.
"My dad lived through a couple of accidents. . . . He was covered up in a roof fall once. Another time, he had one of the
worst concussions they'd ever seen, and his head was all cut up
and torn. I always knew there was a possibility of death.

"You're told that if you're going to marry a coal miner, you
might be a widow. And you know that from what you see
growing up. There's no mining camp where everybody don't
know at least one family where someone died or got hurt bad.
You're told, 'Don't talk about it too much,' and 'Don't rock the
boat,' and 'We'll get by if it's God's will.' But you know . . .
that's one thing when you're a child, and another thing if it's
your husband that you're thinking about."

But talking about mining was as natural to the miners as the
deep underground coal seams were to the West Virginia mountains. Coal miners talked about their work at work, at home,
and in their social gatherings. The women said, "The miners
mine more coal in their talk than they ever do in the mine." In-
tentionally and unintentionally in this way miners educated
and informed their families about the nature of mining and the
problems and difficulties of their specific jobs. The social interactions of the immediate family, the extended family, and
friendship networks provided contexts in which even women
who grew up in nonmining families learned about the dangers
and stresses of working underground.

Both Sue and Laura grew up in nonmining families. Sue's
father was a truck driver, and Laura's father managed a small
retail store. They knew, in a surface and general way, that
mining was a dangerous job. Their knowledge of mining was
gained from hearing their parents talk about stories in newspapers and on the radio, from events related by their school

friends, and sometimes, from death or injuries to neighbors or someone known by name in another neighborhood.

Sue married a miner shortly before she graduated from high school, more than twenty years before our interview. Her husband had always worked in the mines, and, when we talked to her, she had two adult sons, a son-in-law, and a brother who worked in the mines as well. Her family was not pleased that she was going to marry a miner, and they warned her that the probability that she would be a young widow was high. Sue said, "I didn't believe it then because I didn't really know anything about mining. I don't think it would have kept me from getting married, but I had a lot to learn."

Laura's perception of mining families was strongly colored by her mother's ideas about mining families who "lived back in the holler, were frequently unemployed, spent their money foolishly, and failed to educate their children." At nineteen, Laura married a young carpenter who worked for a local building contractor. Shortly after Laura became pregnant with their first child, her husband was laid off from his carpentry job. After a month of finding no work for his carpentry skills, he went into the mines. It was not the only job to be found but was the only one that would pay enough to support a family Laura's mother was upset, but Laura told her, "You can't make any money here any other way. . . . You're either a miner or you're likely not to earn a living."

Sue and Laura were nearly a decade apart in age, but each said the other's stories about learning about mining life were the same as her own. "I began paying more attention to what went on in the newspapers and such, and then, from his very first day, he came home and told me about things. . . . It was the first thing he'd start to talk about, and sometimes we'd still be talking about it when we went to bed. I think I learned everything right along with him. I knew how scared he was when he first went down. He talked about nothing else all night. I know how hard it was to learn to work around, squatting down, and how embarrassed he was to ask questions. I always heard when he learned something new and what he learned to pay attention to."

Sue said, "I knew nothing about mining when I married. Oh, you read about it. You hear about it. But the first impact that really catches you hard after you're married is the first mining accident. One time when he came home, he was nervous, and he said there was a fire in his section. Later I thought, 'What if the extinguishers didn't work? What if the power didn't go off? What if there was an explosion?' Then the worry started to develop. Then you think, 'That can happen to us, to him.' You begin to feel how hazardous, dangerous it is, and you begin to feel you just have to be constantly prepared for the worst."

Laura said her first realization of what the dangers of mining could mean to her came when her husband's brother died in a nearby mine explosion and fire. She said that, for a while, her husband thought he might not go back. "They never found all the bodies. He got a little crazy about it. He talked about it all the time, and I think he told me every word he heard about everything that went on and everything he thought. He was so upset about it, he dreamed about it . . . and he said he'd never go back again. I hoped and prayed he'd stay out but after a month he went back. I think he got over it more than I did. I was the calm one at first, but I still think about it, and I think he's put it away."

Sue and Laura, like many of the other miners' wives who took part in our conversations, were particularly fearful of the dangers of fires, falling rocks, and explosions. To a slightly lesser degree, they also feared electrocution, the mining machinery, and the deadly gasses that accumulated in pockets within the mines. Their fears were realistic: falling rocks from the roofs and sides of shafts, fires from many sources, and explosions have been the major causes of death in the mines. The state's records over the years from 1897 to 1987 show that miners were subject to extreme risk from roof falls, fires, and explosions. Electrocution, machinery accidents, and exposure to deadly gasses were less frequent causes of death but were, and have remained, constant threats to the lives of miners (State of West Virginia 1988).

Laura said, "What I learned right away is there are two main hazards, fires and falls. Those are the two ways you get trapped and killed. He's already been in two fires. You feel that for a long time. You're waiting all the time for a fall or a fire, and it's on your mind because you know eventually something like this is going to happen whether he gets hurt or not. It's going to happen. That's the kind of work it is.

"You have to be prepared. When he goes to work, I know how long it takes to get there and how long he takes before he goes down. And, as long as he's there, he's on my mind. When the phone rings, I wonder, 'Should I answer it or shouldn't I?' The first thing that comes to your mind is 'What's happened in the mine?' When he's on night shift and the phone rings at night, I hear it in my sleep, and I sit up, and there's this awful feeling. . . . It takes me a couple of minutes to be able to get up and answer it. Then, it takes me a while to get back to sleep again, and what goes on in my mind is 'What if?'

"It affects the kids too. They hear their dad talking about what happens in the mine, and they hear other people talking about it. They worry about it. When Billy says his prayer at night, he says, 'God, please don't let the mine fall in on daddy and don't let there be another fire.' Sally's older and she takes it different, but I can see her listen and get quiet when he talks about a close call. She doesn't say much, but the kind of questions she asks let you know she knows. She was old enough to remember how he was when his brother was killed, and it scared her, the way he was. The first night he went back, she cried, so you see, it's in the kids' minds."

Nancy was familiar with mining when she married, but she said, "You keep on learning about it right along with him. Where he is now, it's low coal. . . . Well, I know what low coal is, but this is the first time he's worked it. In the highest places he can't stand. They work mostly crawling, duckwalking, you know. They had a cave-in when he was working up front on the miner. There's no support up there at the miner, and there's only forty-five inches of coal in the seam. He has to duckwalk everywhere, and he said, 'I was goin' as fast as I could go, and it was comin' down right behind me as I went.' When I heard him say that, I felt like my heart stopped. I couldn't sleep that night or the next couple either. All I could see was him under there not getting out.

"A couple of our friends got killed at Blacksville. You feel it for a long time, and you know that eventually something like this is likely to happen. . . . That's the kind of work it is. You don't want to hear about it but you do. His brother was on the mine rescue team when they rescued the men at Blacksville. He told us about the bodies falling apart when you picked them up. That affects you for the rest of your life. I never expected anything like that, but that don't make any difference. My friend's from a mining family, and she never expected it, but her husband's dead."

Laura echoed the words of the other women. "If a woman says she doesn't worry, she's lying. You feel like you have to be prepared. As soon as they go to work . . . during that time they are constantly on your mind. You know that's where they are, underground, and you're just prepared. When the phone rings, you wonder, 'Should I answer it or shouldn't I answer it?' That's the first thing that comes to your mind, 'What's happened in the mines?' It's a little cloud that's there in the back of your mind. You can't do anything about it. . . . I don't think it ever ends. It's never going to change."

While Sue, Laura, and Nancy were not familiar with the records that are kept on the number of fatalities in the mines, they risked a guess of "more than ten thousand." But since the beginning of large-scale mining, more than twenty thousand miners have died in the process of "earning a living the only way you can around here." With a few exceptions, all of the mines have been the site of fatalities, and the names of the mines where major disasters have occurred are an index to the dark and bloody history of mining. The list of major mine disasters is long, even when reduced to just those incidents in which there were large numbers of fatalities: Monongah, 1907, 361 men; Jed, 1912, 80 men; Eccles, 1914, 183 men; Layland, 1915, 112 men; Benwood, 1924, 119 men; Everettville, 1927, 97 men. The list could go on into the present (State of West Virginia 1986, 19).

The names of these mines and their message of the dangers of mining have a familiarity that is more than just a part of the written history of mining. The major mining tragedies are shocking reminders of the losses that have occurred in many mining families over the generations. About half of the women interviewed had lost a family member, friend, acquaintance, or neighbor to mining accidents. Their losses and those of the other mining families they knew combined with their knowledge of the nature of mining and of the working conditions in the mines to heighten their perceptions of mining's dangers.

Even the most realistic fears about the dangers of mining were colored and made more ominous by the fact that, when an accident occurred, what had happened might be unknown to all but those who lay dead or dying under the ground. Families, and sometimes even rescue workers, were cut off from those below. Mary said, "It's a feeling you can't describe. . . . You don't know if they are suffocating, if they've been cut, crushed, burned. You don't know any of that. . . . You can't get in. Nobody tells you because nobody knows. . . . You wait. They're underground, and you don't know if they're dead or alive.

"It's something you can't know about unless you've been standing there. . . . Everyone is there. . . . Everyone knows it might be their people down there. All you can do is pray. Sometimes they just bring them out and they're dead. I was there when they brought out my brother dead. I was there when they brought Tom [Mary's husband] out all bloody. Or maybe you just never see them again. . . . You might get a belt buckle . . . or their lunch bucket . . . or nothing . . . and you don't want to think why."

Amy and Flo were both widowed by accidents in the mines. The tragedy that miners' wives feared so greatly interrupted their lives and changed them forever. Amy's husband died in the mines several years before we met. In her early forties when we talked, she thought she might remarry someday but said she would not marry a miner again. He grandfather died in the mines, her uncle died of black lung, and her father-in-law would have to retire early because of the disease. Although she was the third generation of a mining family, she said it would end with her. She would not allow her son to go into the mines and if he should insist on becoming a miner, she would do everything in her power to keep him out of the mines, she said.

Flo was widowed by a mine accident over a decade ago. Raised in a mining family, she said, "When you marry a miner, you know what to expect, but you pray it won't happen to you." She married another miner a few years after her first husband died because "that's who you know around here, who you see at church and at the store, and if you go out anywhere. I said I wouldn't marry a miner again, but a woman has to put her life back together again. You have to make friends, have to do for your kids, keep on going. And this is where my life is."

The circumstances of their husbands' deaths differed. Flo's husband was killed in a roof fall, and Amy's husband suffocated, or "at least, that's what they said." Amy said she was told that when her husband was trapped by a roof fall, his respirator eventually gave out and he inhaled gas and just went to sleep. She said she tried not to think of it, but despite her efforts, "It would come back over and over again. . . . Even now I think about him almost every day. There's just times when even now it's hard to keep it out of my mind.

"He didn't start out in the mines even though his family did, so he used to come home and talk a lot about his work. I worried, and after he had been covered up once in a roof fall, I worried even more. He was all right that time, not even injured badly. He told me, 'After the roof fell, they just kept digging and clawing and digging until they go to me.' He said, 'I was lucky that time.' I hated hearing him say that because I worried about what could happen and him not be lucky. He just laughed at me when I said that . . . not to be mean, just to get me not to be worried about it. He was more affectionate than most men, and if he thought I worried then he worried, so he always tried to . . . well, get me out of my worries."

Amy heard from other miners that on the day her husband died the foreman "noticed there was a crack in the ceiling, but he didn't bother to say anything about it because in his mind it wasn't bad." After the ceiling fell, the people in the mine office called Amy's mother by mistake, and she went to Amy's house. "You'd better come," her mother said, "There's been an accident." They went to the mine together and waited outside the big fence for hours. But the miners were buried deep, and it was the next day before Amy was told there was no hope of recovering her husband alive. Others were down there as well. Days turned into weeks before they recovered the bodies. "They wouldn't let me see him, and they said nothing was recovered with the bodies, not a lunch bucket, a boot, a watch, a wallet, or any personal effects."

Amy said the mine company never reopened the section where her husband died. When she asked if they couldn't open it just enough to find something of her husband's that she might have, they told her it was not possible. But different officials told different stories, and it seemed so strange that she did not believe them. One person told her the way was blocked, another said the roof was bad, and a third group said in writing there was a lot of gas in that area that could not be ventilated, and even the machinery had been abandoned.

She said she was bothered by the secretiveness of the company men she talked to. They said it was a fall, they put this in writing, and they showed her the first report that came from the supervisor. But when she told that to some of the other miners who had worked on her husband's shift and asked them about it, "They just looked at each other and said there was nothing I could do. . . . I couldn't bring him back and I should forget about it. They said, 'Leave it. No one can do anything about it now.'"

For more than a year Amy kept her husband's personal things exactly as they were. His toothbrush was in the bathroom holder, his razor on the bathroom sink, his clothes in the closet, and his slippers under the bed. "I couldn't believe he was gone. I couldn't even say he was dead even to myself. There was a funeral, but it didn't seem real to me. Everyone was very nice—neighbors, friends, minister, other miners. Everyone wanted to help if they could. It was just all so terribly wrong, because I knew he was dead but I kept thinking, he just couldn't be. He just went to work like any other day.

"I think I was a little crazy that year, and—it was funny—because everyone thought I was taking it well. Even the minister thought I was going all right, and he stopped coming up when I stopped going to church. One of his [her husband's] friends said he never knew someone to handle all this and all the legal stuff [Amy filed a complaint against the coal company] so well. He said my husband would of been proud of me. My mom and dad knew better and they worried and his dad worried. He'd come up here and sit across the table, and we'd just sit there . . . sometimes not even talking."

Amy said her son would never go into the mines. "He can be anything else he wants, even a ballet dancer," and she smiled a little when she said that. "But I mean every word. I'll do anything to keep him out of the mine. I want to get a better education, maybe go to college, so I can get a better job and send him to college somewhere. I want to move too, go live somewhere else, but that's like a dream. I don't know where I could go or what I could do. It's not right yet. I mean, I feel like I'm not a whole person yet. There's still something missing in me."

Flo was married at fifteen, a mother at eighteen, and a widow at twenty-five. She said she and her husband were a wild young couple for quite a while, but having a baby settled them both down. They had someone else to live for then. Neither of them worried much about his job until the baby was born, but then "We started to think about what it would mean if he got hurt and couldn't work, or if he got killed and there was just me to take care of us. He did get hurt once and couldn't work for a week, and we could see how fast we went through what we had. I guess we saw that an accident would mean more than just not having any money to spend on Saturday night."

Flo said the things she had learned as a child came back to her then: the way her mother had worried about her father, the circumstances of a relative's death, a fire in her father's section. "The mine is more hazardous than any other job because they're down there under the ground, and if anything happens, they might not have any way to escape. Anything can happen. It's dark, it's dangerous, and you never know what will happen or when. I remembered my mother looking at the clock nearly every day when it was time for my father to come home. I remembered her standing in the window looking out, waiting. . . . She never said much but we sort of sensed it . . . that she was worried."

She said her memories of her husband's death were as alive when we spoke as they were when he died. One summer afternoon she looked out her window and saw a pickup truck full of men drive into her driveway. When the men got out, she saw it was the foreman and some other miners. They were in their working clothes and still black from the dust. When Flo opened the door, they came into the living room, and the foreman held her hand and told her her husband was dead. A roof fall, they said. It wasn't anyone's fault, they said. No one else had been hurt. A big chunk of the roof just fell down on him.

"I can close my eyes and see them standing at my door. They just stood there and I knew. . . . I knew when I saw them coming up the walk. It was like a hand grabbed me inside, and I didn't want to go open that door. I felt like I couldn't breathe, and they told me I got white as paper before they even started to talk. Then I just screamed."

Flo was hysterical for a while, and the foreman thought they should take her to the hospital; but one of the men called her mother and sister, and they came to the house to take care of her. At the funeral, Flo thought her husband's face looked as though he were asleep; but the satin cover was pulled all the way up to his neck, and he never slept that way. She wanted to fold it down some; but they wouldn't let her touch it, and her mother told her, "They said you don't want to see." Flo said those words stayed in her mind for weeks afterward.

There seemed to be nothing to be done about the accident, and Flo said she believed the men when they said it wasn't anybody's fault. Her husband had been working in a section of the mine where they were putting roof bolts in. A rock the size of a small car came down on him and pinned him against the wall. One of his friends was on the same shift, and he told her he had to have died instantly from the way the rock hit him. His friend told her that her husband probably never even knew anything was going to happen. When she remembered him lying in the casket, it was a comfort to her, she said, to remember that he probably had not known it was going to happen.

Her mother stayed with her for a while; but Flo's stepfather and her youngest sister were still at home to be taken care of, and eventually her mother went home. It was necessary for her to earn an income, so she made arrangements for child care and got a job. She said, "It was better for me that I did have to work because life has to go on, even when you don't want it to. If I could have stayed home, I don't think I would've gotten over it for a long time. And maybe I would've been out there running around and being wild. . . . You don't know what you'll do to help yourself get over something like this."

A few years later she met a man at a church get-together, and when he asked her to marry him, she said, "Yes." Her new husband told her in a general way what was going on in the mine day by day, but, at her request, he did not tell her everything. "I don't think I want to know. I can't handle it really. . . . If I let it, it can just get on my mind so bad that I can't get it off. I just have to do something to make it go away or I'll just be a crying mess. I read my Bible and I pray because you never know what's going to happen. All you can do is pray . . . and that's what I do. I pray."

Mine accidents have caused many fatalities, but roof falls, rib rolls, fires, gas, and explosions are only the immediate threats to life. The long-term threats of black lung (pneumoconiosis), tuberculosis, arteriosclerosis, cancer, and ulcers have given mining a life-threatening status unequaled by any other occupation. As of 1974, coal miners died at twice the rate of other manual workers; their mortality rate from respiratory diseases alone was four times that of the general population, and it was estimated that one out of every ten miners would die from black lung alone (Althouse 1974, 50).

Victims of black lung have not necessarily spent a lifetime working in the mines. There appears to be a range of vulnerability to the cinderlike particles of dust that accumulate in the lungs, and the susceptibility of a given individual cannot be predicted. Some people can work in the mines for years before they display any of the effects of black lung or other respiratory diseases, and some may never experience any significant effects. Others can become partially affected by the dust in the mines in a relatively short time: a few years may bring on respiratory disease symptoms. It is, as one woman said, "a gamble," but everyone acknowledges that miners' chances of being able to work to retirement get smaller with each additional year they spend breathing in the coal and rock dust.

In other countries, mine operators and governments officially recognized the relationship between mine dust and black lung and other respiratory diseases decades ago. Yet over and over through the years, American mine operators, medical practitioners, and the American government denied that the black dust in the mines was harmful to the miners. Years of legal pressure, legislative pressure, and dogged persistence by the miners and their families were necessary before the government acted to establish compensation for miners disabled by black lung.

Dramatic evidence of the pervasiveness of black lung and the need for some form of compensation was presented in the seven years following the passage of the Federal Coal Mine Health and Safety Act in 1969. In those seven years, 225,000 miners were declared totally and permanently disabled as the result of black lung. The number of miners disabled by black lung exceeded the number of Americans who died in the Vietnam War. In addition, 140,000 widows whose husbands had died from black lung were found to qualify for the new act's benefits. Even then, those afflicted by the disease were likely to spend months, and sometimes years, entangled in the red tape of bureaucracy before receiving financial compensation (Smith 1987; Witt and Dotter 1979).

All of the women knew miners with black lung, and, in most of the several-generation mining families, the lives of at least one relative and often several had been appreciably shortened by the breath-depriving disease. Ginny's feelings about black lung were typical of young miners' wives. Her husband was twenty-seven, and Ginny worried about his health in the years ahead. Her worry was more than an occasional moment of concern about an early heart attack, high blood pressure, or other health conditions that might concern any married woman.

"His dad has black lung, and I worry, 'Is he going to be in the shape his dad is in now?' His dad gets a pension but he's sick and he can't enjoy it. . . . He can't do any of the things he likes to do. . . . What kind of life is that? And he isn't old, only in his late fifties. He hasn't worked for five years, so you see he wasn't old. He hadn't worked a lifetime. It was all the dust and dirt he breathed in. My husband, now he's got this job where he's right at the face where all the dust is. Once in a while he gets to coughing, but he's never yet got the bad coughing spells.

"My friend, Sheila, tells me her husband gets to coughing and has to go into the bathroom, and when it comes up, it's nothing but pure coal dust. He's been in the mine longer. Well, I've never seen my husband do this. . . . There's black dirt when he blows his nose, but he don't cough it up. But . . . I look in time and every year that goes by, it's building up. I've got two uncles and they're just like his dad . . . constant coughing . . . not able to work, living like they're really old. And I think, 'Will this be him in time? Is he going to be sitting in front of the TV and on the front porch not able to do anything?'"

Another young wife, Karen, said that her husband had been working in the mines only seven years, but she believed it was inevitable that he would get black lung. "It really gets me. He's been in the mines for seven years, and every day it's coal dust in his nostrils, lungs, hair, clothes, eyes, ears. You know that if he's down there, he's breathing it in all day, and he just has to have a bit of it [black lung] by now. It don't go away once it's in there. He comes home and tells me, 'So and so had a checkup, and they found out he has black lung already.' Some of them haven't even been there as long as he has.

"It's so ironic. He's working in the mine so we can have a good home and good retirement and all. But working in the mine is killing him, and he likely won't make it to retirement. We talk about it, but I can't help but think about how what he's doing for us may be making it impossible for him to be able to have a good life when he's older. I can't resolve my feelings about it. . . . I can't control it. It makes me feel angry and frustrated. It's just not right. I don't know what to do about it, and I try to shelve it, but it still bothers me. He says that's just the way it is, but I can't accept that. It's not supposed to be that way."

Mary's husband began to experience the symptoms of black lung long before it was time for him to retire. She said that at first he just noticed a shortness of breath when he worked at particularly hard jobs. Later he began to feel more tired earlier in the working shift and more short of breath when he pushed himself at work. The cough that he had had for years grew worse. At night he would cough so hard he would wake them both up, and sometimes his cough kept him from falling asleep. The mucus from his lungs was black with coal dust. He told Mary he did not have to have the doctor tell him what was wrong.

Her husband said Mary worried much more about it than he did because she had helped take care of an uncle, after watching him change from a strong, healthy man to a weak, breathless invalid. Her uncle finally died from black lung, and over the years some other relatives died from black lung, emphysema, or lung cancer. Her husband also said he had never thought too much about it while he was working because "there wasn't much a miner could do about it." He also said he never really believed, as some miners still do, that chewing tobacco or gum would prevent the dust from getting down into his lungs. "I figured I'd get it or I wouldn't, and there were more dangerous things to worry about each day."

Mary's husband finally retired on black-lung disability, but the years of breathing in the microscopic, sharp-edged particles of coal and rock dust had done more than fill his lungs with dust. His condition grew worse; the diagnosis was lung cancer. He then spent his time at home doing what he could with his severely limited breathing capacity. He watched television but did not really like it very much. He talked to Mary, the neighbors dropped in often, and his children frequently came to spend an afternoon or evening. Mary tried to make the time pass as easily and happily as possible. They both knew there was not much time left for him, and they did not want to talk about it very much.

Helen's husband worked in the mines for more than twenty years before the damage to his lungs became so debilitating that he could no longer do the heavy work. Despite his obvious breathing problems, his twenty-two years of work as a miner, and the coal-black mucus that came out of his lungs when he coughed, the doctors who reviewed the cases of miners filing black-lung disability claims could not agree on whether or not he had black lung. He was denied disability benefits. He needed a job and went back to the coal company, but they refused to hire him because of the doctors' statements about his lung condition.

Later, when the company was in great need of experienced miners, he was allowed to go back to work. He worked for a few more years and then, too ill to continue, tried again to get black-lung disability. The reviewing physicians did not need to go through their procedures again. This time the doctors were sure he had black lung, but, as was always the case, the paperwork took a long time. Fifteen days after he died, the black-lung pension approval came through.

Helen looked back at their life together and felt sad about how ignorant she and her husband had been about the disease. "If I'd known about this black lung from the first, I'd have made him get out of there. He didn't know either. I mean, people generally didn't know. . . . You knew men got bad lungs, coughed up dirt. He knew that, but we didn't know how many got black lung . . . or how many got lung cancer. We knew when the mines was out, he felt better, didn't cough as much and all. But we just thought it was the hard work and all. When the mines was out [on strike], he slept better and didn't get as tired, and if he was out for more than a week or so, the cough would go away.

"The doctors didn't know either or they didn't let on. They always told him it was his heart, and they never said it was his lungs even when he told them how he'd cough up so much dirt. Later it even hurt to draw breath, but they never said 'black lung' to him or me. But he inhaled enough of that dust and everything to affect his lungs, and he really did have the black lung. He was sick a lot those years, dragging himself off to that mine when he could hardly do anything but work and try to rest. He never had a prime of life. The mines took it away from him."

One expression of the stress the miners experienced as they worked day to day in deep and dangerous surroundings was their almost constant preoccupation with their tasks and equipment, with the nature of the sections they worked in the mine, and with their coworkers, their supervisors, and the company. Helen recalled that her husband "couldn't relax until he'd gone through the whole day. I knew everything about that company over there and what they did and who said what and how his day went. I knew how many cars he'd loaded, how many timbers he'd put in, how much coal they hustled. I always knew when a car'd run away because when he'd come home . . . he'd lost his voice trying to warn the men.

"Nothing was kept secret. . . . I heard about the explosions and rocks falling and accidents. I knew who it was got hurt and who brought them out . . . when there was an accident. I heard it over and over. He always worried about things, and if I hadn't listened, he might have been one of those that drinks. But I was always here, and I heard everything. I know the fear they have . . . I have . . . of being down there. I heard my father tell of the sounds they hear and how they listen for things. . . . Certain sounds can mean things.

"I heard my brothers talk about everything just like he [her husband] did. I saw them come out hurt more than once, and we all heard about that . . . everything. It's all inside them and talking gets it out . . . you know. Everyone knows that . . . when you've been through something, you have to talk about it. The mine is like that. It's never safe. When I was just little, my father always talked to my mother about how things were and how he felt. I saw how my mother worried, but she wanted to know and I wanted to know. I had to know what went on every day, and they have to talk about it too."

Laura's husband occasionally had chest pains, and she thought the pain was due to stress. "He has a dangerous job, more than most do. He and his buddy are like a team that gets the mine prepared for the other men to come in.

"He tells me what's going on in the mines, but sometimes I'd rather not hear. . . . I've heard too much . . . and so he doesn't always tell me everything. But he needs to talk about it . . . like everybody does, I guess. But more than most because this job's not like working in a store or driving a truck. I can see when he wants to talk, and I feel like something, like some wall or something, wants to go up inside. But I see how tired he is, how this hurts and that hurts, and I know it helps him to just get it out, talk about it. I wish he could work somewhere else, but he says he's used to it. I don't think anyone ever gets used to it. I don't think he does even if he says so. A friend of mine says if you're raised in a mining family, it's easier to get used to, but I never got used to it. . . . I don't know how anybody can. It's not the kind of thing you can get used to no matter where you grow up."

Whether or not being raised in mining families had prepared the women, and whether or not they wanted to hear the miners' stories, the conditions of mining were a part of the environment in which all of them lived. Each felt she would have changed these conditions if she could have; and they talked about how, if things were different, their lives would benefit. Yet they would not have changed their husbands' choice of work if their husbands did not wish it. Instead, they worked at making family routines as stable as possible, at coping with their feelings, and at finding strength and enjoyment in the company of family and friends.

Nevertheless, they experienced an uneasiness in their daily lives that was reflected in their conversations. They felt an anxious sense of waiting when they heard stories of other miners' deaths and injuries and a sense of foreboding, an early warning uneasiness about the kind of loss that might come from respiratory diseases. They worked to suppress thoughts about what actually could happen to their husbands deep beneath the earth, but their daily efforts to cope did no more than create a wary truce between the women and the nature of their husbands' occupation. It seemed to be as Sue said, "It's the men work in the mines, but it's the women carry the mines in them."

FOUR

Living Day by Day:
Women's Work
and Widowhood

Life-threatening accidents resulting from the specific dangers of mining—the roof falls, explosions, and deadly gasses—nearly always had a high probability of occurring and were, in addition, unpredictable and uncontrollable. Because of this, they imposed high levels of stress on mining families and shaped and colored the families' daily home routines. Nevertheless, in most ways, the mining families' daily concerns were similar to those of nonmining families. Adults in both types of families had to fit into their schedules the tasks of homemaking, child rearing, and participating in family events, and they had to divide tasks between wives and husbands.

The difference between the mining families and most other families lay in the impact of the miner's working conditions on all of the tasks, responsibilities, and activities of the family. In many mining families, both in West Virginia and in other mining areas (Scott 1988), the primary intent behind the development of daily routines was to create a home atmosphere that would be beneficial to the miner or, at the very least, not add to the physical and psychological stress of working in the mine. Home and family responsibilities were organized with care so that the miner could be relieved of extra work or worry. Contemporary ideas about the importance of women's careers or a more equitable sharing of home and child-rearing tasks between husbands and wives usually took second place to the notion, "When he's down there, he can't be thinking of what's going on here at home."

In many respects Ginny, Karen, and Lynn were representative of the younger and early middle-aged women, while Mary,

Beth, and Flo were representative of the older women. All six of
the women's husbands had begun working in the mines when
they were in early or late adolescence. Lynn's husband had just
turned sixteen when he went into the mines, and the older
women's husbands had been even younger. They all married
young and started their families soon after marriage. They
shared the common experiences of working when necessary,
juggling the double workload of outside employment and
homemaking, and worrying about their husbands.

Together, the six women's experience as wives, mothers, and
homemakers covered a period stretching from the days when
mining was done with hand tools and men worked alone in
their own sections of the mine to the 1980s when teams of
men used modern mining machinery. Mary, Beth, and Flo had
seen new mining procedures replace the old and had listened to
their husbands' critiques of the new methods. They had listened to explanations of new safety procedures and new safety
equipment, and they believed that the new ways could save
lives if the men observed them.

Ginny, Karen, and Lynn knew that deaths and injuries in the
mines were much more frequent in the days when Mary's,
Beth's, and Flo's husbands began mining than they were when
we talked. They, too, had listened to their husbands tell about
safety equipment and safety procedures, and they had heard the
men say that many miners never used the new equipment or
followed the procedures. The equipment was awkward and uncomfortable, the procedures were time-consuming, and the
miners were always under pressure to produce. The younger
women were just as concerned for their husbands as the older
women had been for theirs in earlier years, despite the now
lower frequency of mining deaths and injuries. Younger and
older alike knew that deep mining still claimed more lives than
did other occupations.

There was general agreement with Lynn's statement that
"Your whole life gets involved in keeping him safe. You don't
tell him that you can't sleep at night or when things aren't going
quite right at home. You can't take a chance on having him
worry about anything but his job when he's down there. You

keep the house, make it be a pleasant home, and make him as comfortable at home as you can. You do things you wouldn't do if he worked at a different job . . . even if he just worked outside the mine or was a company man or like that."

Mary said, "In my mind, there's no such thing as fifty-fifty marriages when he's a coal miner. It's more like seventy-five–twenty-five, and it was the same way with my mother, my sisters, and everyone. All of them catered to their husbands. A woman has got to tell her husband what she needs too. But it's just that with his job and all, you got to make it easy for him at home. You might want him to be the one who has to deal with the children's problems, and you might want to wait until he gets home to put a lot on him, but you can't. He can't have no worries or angers on his mind when he goes down there to work.

"You can't change it, not if you want to live here, and not if you want to make more than in a store. . . . There might be a couple jobs that pay more but not without an education, and when he was young, there wasn't any. You just have to accept some of these things because you have to have a livelihood and that's that. No work nowhere can be compared to going down in the mine. You have to get used to having your husband come home so tired he can't do anything. You got to get used to him being so dirty it don't come out of his skin. Or having him come home sometimes with a wrenched back or smashed fingers or telling you that someone you know got hurt today and he's lucky it wasn't him. You got to do more for him."

Beth reflected, "I never wanted to marry a miner, but he couldn't find a job anywhere else. Being a miner's wife means you have less time than maybe some other wives because you want to do as much as you can to keep the load off him. His work is physically hard. It's dangerous. It's not like working in a store or teaching school or driving a truck. It just wouldn't be right to have him have to carry the load at home too, carry that on his shoulders. I take care of most things. . . . I'm the banker. I'm the planner. Big decisions we talk about, but pretty much I make the decisions about things around the house. I always took care of the kids, took them to school, saw they did their homework. He helps out when he can, of course, but I don't want him to do too much. His job is too hard as it is."

The methods the women used to relieve their husbands of extra work or concern about household and family matters included more than taking responsibility for the larger share of tasks and decisions. They also took the time and made the effort to insure that their husbands' working days were free of any discomforts they could have foreseen. They paid extra attention to selecting food for the lunches their husbands carried down into the mine and to maintaining their work clothing. Some of the women cooked or baked special things their husbands enjoyed or made them special meals before they went to work.

Ginny and Karen acknowledged the importance of "taking on the major share of lots of things that have to be done around a home," but they also felt that doing little things to help their husbands was important. Ginny said, "I keep his clothes all fixed, you know, so there's no rips or tears to catch on anything. . . . The knees get wore out fast, and I keep them mended, so it's more comfortable when he has to get down. He's going to be down on his knees on rocks and wet, and he says the padding really helps. I take old work clothes and cut them up and use them for extra padding in some of the ones where the knees are thin. I keep everything in his lunch bucket that he wants in just the way he wants it. I've even gotten up early in the morning sometimes, so I can fix something special for him. I don't want to think about it, but you never know when something can happen, and you want to do anything you can for him . . . just for him alone, you know. There's nothing else you can do."

Karen was one of the few women who had gone down in the mine on a company tour to see what it's like to work beneath the ground. She said, "I guess I was sort of doubtful if it was as bad as you hear, but when I got down there, I knew I couldn't do that every day. It's so dark. . . . You never realize how dark it is in a mine, and there's just little lights. And the roof's right over your head. . . . You can just put out your hand and touch it. There's no room even in the one they just keep for show.

There's the rock right over your head, and the whole mountain's on top of it. And it's noisy, you know. There's so much noise from the belts and miners, you can't hear, and then in the ones where they're not working, there's all kinds of funny noises down there. He laughed at me, but I didn't like it.

"I feel like there's not much I can do as far as making him safer down there but keep his clothes in good shape, pack his bucket just right. I even made him a special mine bag to carry things in. I know other miners' wives, and they feel the same way. I know what it's like down there. It's dark and wet and cold, and, well, I couldn't do it. There's men who go down there and turn around and come back up. . . . They can't do it. . . . Some don't even last one day. He always says he doesn't mind the dark and all, but I'm not sure. If doing these little things makes it better for him down there, then I want to do it."

Nearly all of the women believed it was necessary to try to keep husbands free of worry and make them comfortable while they were working. But more difficult and more stressful tasks were their attempts to accommodate marriage relationships, child rearing, and homemaking to their husbands' rotating work shifts.

Laura had never liked coping with her husband's rotating-shift work but said, "I tried different ways, but it finally seemed best to change with him, so everything changes when he changes. His family thinks it's crazy, but it never worked to have us all be on our own schedule, while he was on ours only once in every couple months. I don't like this way much, but I figure it's better for him and for us. It's the only way that we can spend more than a couple of weeks out of each couple months together like a family, and it's important that he gets to spend as much time with us as we can get.

"Now, the kids' sleeping time never changed much—they needed a regular sleeping time when they were little—but mine changed some, the meals changed, and time together changed. But when we do have time together, I can't always be cheerful and happy about it because it's not right for me. I can't always get used to it. It's really hard to fit our schedule in with normal schedules like for shopping and church and things like that, but if we want to see him, we have to. I don't know of anybody that likes shift work. It makes problems for every family."

Ginny was also unhappy with her husband's shift schedule. She made fewer changes in the family schedule than Laura, but like the majority of the women, tried to fit homemaking tasks and her personal needs into the changing shift hours. "I try to work around his shift. Well, I have to is the way it is. Night shift's the worst. Mostly I get the things done while he's not sleeping like cleaning and stuff. If he's working at night and sleeping in the day, I clean while he's gone and do the laundry and things . . . But I don't like cleaning and doing the laundry and all at night. . . . That means I can't do anything else.

"If I don't do that, we don't get any time together when he is awake. If he's sleeping in the day, I take the baby and do the shopping. It just makes it hard to do everything. I can't have anyone in while he's sleeping—he doesn't sleep well, really ever except at night—and he can't babysit for me so I can go out. Sometimes I get so lonely I think I'll cry. We can't do anything on a regular schedule. When he's on night shift, sometimes nothing goes right for me at home because he's trying to sleep in the day, and if he can't, then I get upset. If the baby's fussy, I have to keep her quiet or take her over to my mother's house, and she's not really close. I just hate to think of it always being like this, living around the clock."

Rotating shifts created heavy strains for all of the women whether or not they tried to accommodate the family's schedules to the miner's hours. Even the women whose husbands had worked in the mines for many years found the continual adjustments to changing hours a perennially difficult task. Over the years, Cora's and Rose's husbands had occasionally worked on permanent shifts, but most of their husbands' years in the mines had been on rotating shifts. In common with thousands of other long-term shift workers' wives, they believed their husbands' shifts were constant irritants that exaggerated small problems and created new ones as home needs changed, children grew older, and other life events occurred (Mellor 1986; Schwartz and Schwartz 1975).

From Jeanne Rasmusen Collection, East Tennessee State University
Foundation/Archives of Appalachia. Courtesy of Archives and
Special Collections, East Tennessee State University.

The scenes shown in these photographs are representative of the
lives of miners' wives, children, families, and friends from Kentucky and West Virginia. They do not show the women whose
stories are related in this book, who preferred to remain anony-
mous.

The Scotia Mine disaster of 1976 made real the worst fears of all miners' wives—the loss of loved ones. The woman in the photo below mourns a husband who survived Vietnam, only to die in the Eastern Kentucky coalfields. Photos by Earl Dotter.

For those who escape death in the mines, loss of limbs and other injuries remain constant threats that place heavy burdens on miners' families. Jeanne Rasmusen Collection, East Tennessee State University Foundation/Archives of Appalachia. Courtesy of Archives and Special Collections, East Tennessee State University.

The Brookside Mine strike of 1973-74 pitted miners and their families against a powerful mining company in Harlan County, Kentucky, largely in protest against unsafe conditions. When the miners were forbidden to picket the company, their wives took their place on the picket line—and in jail. Photo by Earl Dotter.

Minnie Lunsford, a Harlan County miner's wife, demonstrates her support for miners and their wives arrested for picketing the Brookside Mine. Miners' wives, old and young, are increasingly active in protesting conditions in the mines. Photo by Earl Dotter.

For decades most miners and their families lived in coal camp houses, such as those above. West Virginia Coal Life Project, courtesy of West Virginia State Archives.

Today's mining families mostly live away from the coal camps, but years of hard work to afford a comfortable, modern home like that below are threatened when mines close and workers are unemployed. The burden of mine closings and long strikes often falls heaviest on miners' wives. Photo by John Costello of the *Philadelphia Inquirer*.

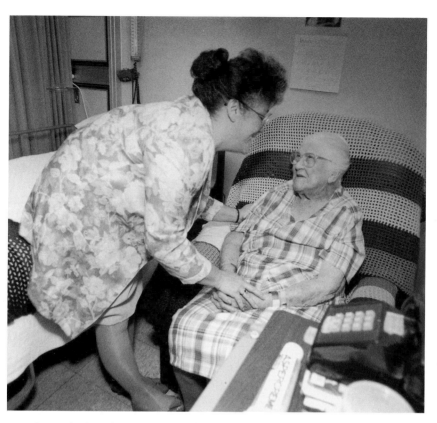

Increasingly, miners' wives are learning to make their own way. This woman is a social work assistant. Photo by John Costello of the *Philadelphia Inquirer*.

West Virginia's children are its primary human resource. Will they choose to follow their grandfathers and fathers, and for some their mothers, into the mines? Photo by John Costello of the *Philadelphia Inquirer*.

"Changing shifts is always pretty hard to live with. When the kids were little, you had to make them be quiet in the daytime and that means maybe they couldn't do what they want in their own house. That's hard, specially when they're little . . . or if you can't handle it. Me not getting to see him when he works nights is hard, and he don't get to see them [the children] except maybe just for a little time before he goes to work or to bed. The kids ask, 'When's daddy going to be here?' and 'Why can't daddy take me?' and I minded being the one who always had to do the taking too.

"If you're working days and he's working nights, you just go by each other night and morning. Sometimes the only time you see him is on weekends. You have to be mother and father a lot of the time too. Even meals is hard. And sometimes it's the little things like that just wear at you. Should I cook for him when he comes home, or cook for us and then for him too, or just let him eat what you had? I don't like it if he don't get what he likes to eat, but I don't like to cook all night either. He don't make as much of it as I do. . . . He says, 'Do what's easy,' but it's complicated. It affects us all because we can't keep a regular schedule unless we want to do things without him, and sometimes it turns out we just don't do anything because it just doesn't fit into his schedule."

Other women, young and old, felt similarly about rotating shifts. Family matters and relationships outside the family were all touched by the constant around-the-clock movement of the miners' working hours. It affected planning and carrying out household tasks, child-rearing responsibilities and activities, social activities outside the immediate family, the occupational choices of the women who worked, and inevitably, the marriage relationship itself. In addition, it added more weight to the women's worries about their husbands' safety in the mines.

The women's worries about their husbands' safety increased the first few days of a new shift. Rose said, "It's a dangerous job on any shift, but working like he does now makes it worse. It takes him almost a week to get used to a new shift. Then it's near time to change again. He doesn't sleep well when he changes shifts, not right away. . . . Then he goes to work tired, and that's when accidents are like to happen. He's come home and told me, 'I almost got hurt,' because he was tired and didn't do something right, or someone else did something wrong because they were tired and not paying attention."

Karen agreed and said, "Night shifts are really bad. That's when I really worry because I know he didn't get enough sleep. I know he's gone down there tired, and I know he worries, too. I can't always take it calmly. Shift work ain't necessary, he says. There's a lot of men want to work steady on all the shifts, so they don't have to keep them rotating. All the miners around here do it, but it doesn't make production better. There's more accidents, and it just doesn't make any sense to make them keep on doing it."

Louise's husband had always worked on rotating shifts. She felt that she not only worried more about him when he worked night shift, but she also worried more about what she would do if something happened at home. "Having him be down there is a worry to me, but when he's down there at night where you can't get to him, can't call him, makes it really bad sometimes. I don't know what I'd do if something happened to the baby or to me. He always says they'd go and get him . . . and maybe they would . . . but it's not like he was on the other end of the telephone. He's down there, he's out of touch, and we're here all by ourselves.

"It's a big worry to me. . . . I think I worry more about things that might go wrong because he's down there . . . just anything, the house, the car, me being sick. Days are bad, but it's night that makes me worry more. I know any kind of trouble can seem worse at night, and I tell myself that, but it only helps a little. And he tells me 'don't worry so,' but when it gets dark and if there's something wrong here then I do worry."

The women always expressed their concerns over their husbands' safety clearly and without coloring them with any suggestion of resentment that their husbands had chosen such dangerous work. Indeed, there was almost unanimous agreement that the local economy and a man's freedom to choose what he would do were the determining issues in his job choice. But their concerns over their husbands' safety and their

desire to take on additional home or child-rearing tasks or to do
special things at home to relieve their husbands of worry over
home matters sometimes combined with shift work problems
to cause underlying resentments about their respective home
responsibilities. Although all but a few of the younger women
generally accepted the traditional division of role responsibilities by gender, these underlying resentments were fairly
common sources of problems between the couples.

Paula had two young children. Her mother wanted her to go
to college, and, Paula said, "it seemed like a good idea. . . . I
didn't know what I wanted to do then, but a college education
gets you farther even here." In her third college semester, she
met the man she would marry, and at the end of her sophomore
year she married and left school. She said, "My family was
upset, but I wanted to take the time off and start our home. My
mother said I'd never get back, and I told her that was silly."
Paula intended to go back the next year, but her first pregnancy
prevented her return. The birth of her second child two and a
half years later meant delaying her education even longer. With
her husband working on rotating shifts, she wondered if she
would ever be able to go to school.

"It isn't that I don't want to do what I can to make his job
easier. I *do* want to do that, but I want something for myself
too, something that's just mine, something where I can go and
do my thing. We talk about going back to school, but there's no
way I can do that . . . even when the kids are older. I don't see
how we could do it with his work the way it is. It's not just the
money. It's the money and the time. I don't like to think that
his work runs us but it does. I don't like to be the one who has
to be mother and father a lot of the time either, take care of
most things, and take care of him too. I really mind that a lot of
the things that two people do together, making the decisions
and things like that, I have to do. Sometimes I think it's too
much, and I feel bad that it might always be like this. I look
ahead and don't see a time when I'll be free of carrying all this."

Ginny had similar feelings, feelings she seldom discussed
with her husband. "A lot of times I get mad, but I don't want to
let him know . . . don't talk about how bad I feel, because I feel

like I have to be there for him. It gets to be a burden thinking
that I have to keep going, have to be strong because he's de-
pending on me. I get really irritable, really grouchy, and
sometimes really depressed. Most everything depends on me.
He'll help if he can on weekends or when they're on strike, but
mostly he doesn't do anything but the things that are too heavy
for me to do. I don't see why I should have to work twenty-four
hours a day, seven days a week just because I was born a
woman. It's his job, and there's nothing I can do about that, but
it's not fair that there's so much on me."

While none of the women with small children worked continuously at full-time employment outside their homes, a few
older women with grown children did have continuing full-time
outside employment. The miners' rotating shifts meant the
women continued to shoulder the major portion of household
tasks in addition to their outside employment responsibilities
even though child-rearing tasks were now over. Evening or
weekend hours to spend with their husbands were even more
limited in these circumstances. Flo worked full time in a restaurant. She would put in long, tiring hours at her work and then
return home to do her housework and extra things to try and
make her husband's job easier.

Each year of their marriage, she took responsibility for yard
work and other outside home-maintenance chores, including
those traditionally thought of as men's chores. In the summer,
Flo put in a garden, weeded and watered it, and preserved the
food grown in it. She laughed at herself and said she was like
the "little red hen in the story that grew the corn and baked
the bread." She believed she was as good at the outside maintenance chores as any man and said there was very little she
could not do from minor plumbing repairs to putting up a
ladder and cleaning out the house gutters. "I can do most anything that needs to be done. Any miners's wife that's been
married for a while has to get used to doing things around the
house if you want to get them done. Not everyone does it but I
think most do.

"I get tired, really tired, and I do ask him to do things. It's not
like he don't want to or just throws it over on me . . . but first I

ask how tired he is or if he has any energy left over. But I do most things. You grow into it. I mean, after so long a time and with a big family like we had, you have to learn how to take care of things whether you're tired or not. A miner's wife works harder than most, I think. . . . You got to keep him going and yourself and your kids. When you got a big problem, you got to solve it by yourself most of the time, so you get used to doing it. I think I got used to it, but it isn't right that that's the way it has to be. It's a problem that you don't know how to solve because it really isn't right. The miner's wife shouldn't have to be doing all the things she does, but then how can he be doing a fifty-fifty share when he's got to work down there? . . . His work is harder than most too, so what do you do?

"Both of my sons are in the mine, and one of them's wife works, and she says she won't do everything . . . He's got to do his share. He doesn't like it, but I tell him she's right. They talked about it and argued when she first said that, and they still argue about it sometimes. He thinks she ought to do like I do, and she says she works all day too, and she isn't going to do everything at home. I think she's right, and I say so, and that's what he don't like. But I told him a woman's got to have some life of her own. If I had it to do all again, I don't think I'd take on all I did, but I can't say that for sure, because it's different now than it was when their dad went into the mine."

While the majority of the women accepted the extension of their responsibilities as a legitimate consequence of their husbands' jobs and the constant rotation of working hours, a few younger women disagreed. They saw themselves and their husbands as differing little from other couples with homes and children and physically arduous, although less dangerous, jobs. While they recognized the dangers of mining and experienced the same stresses of worry and anxiety over the possibility of accidents and death as other miners' wives, they did not feel that they must or should extend their responsibilities to include most of those of their husbands.

Carrie said, "There's nothing really that I can do except psychologically support him. . . . I can't make his job any easier. I can only listen, tell him to do his best. It's just a job. I know it's a hard job, but he wanted to do it, and I don't think that has to mean that I've go to do everything at home. Some do. I think most of my friends do, but I don't. I don't try to hide our problems from him. I think if I did, he would be even more worried, wondering what was wrong. He's not just a miner. He's a father, a husband. And we have our problems, too. I do take most of the responsibilities for the house but he shares some. I'm studying for a job where I'll be self-employed, and one of these days I'll be working. And then he'll have to do more . . . and he has to expect it. He can't expect me to do everything."

Several of the younger women pointed out that their husbands had chosen to work in the mine rather than be employed at a lower wage elsewhere or go to another town. Karen said her husband did not want to move away from the area where his family lived, even though, at the time of their marriage, he could have found work in a nearby state and would have been only a few hours away from home. Then too his closest friends had gone into the mines, and they had talked about the money that could be made in the mine. She said she thought sometimes it was like they wanted to make it seem exciting to him. Karen and her husband had discussed the dangers of mining and the difficulty of working rotating shifts, before he went into the mine. Because they both came from mining families and had friends who were miners, they had seen at first hand the problems that arose in families because of the dangers of mining, the frequent unemployment, and the stress of rotating shifts.

"He wanted to go in. I did everything to talk him out of it. I even cut out ads from papers about other jobs and stuck them around the house. I do worry about him, about what can happen, whether he'll get black lung, get crushed under a pile of rock, get burned like one of his friends did, all that. You know it's all possible, but it's something he does, something he wants to do. I didn't want him to go into the mines but that's what he wanted to do. I have to live with it, the kids have to live with it, and there's nothing I can do about it. Some of my friends do everything for their husbands, but I won't do that. He's got to help too, even when he's working a bad shift.

"We don't really have any big problems about it because he doesn't mind doing things when he's home. He'll pick up, help with lunch, do things around the house. He grew up in a big family, and everybody had to do their share. He never had to do housework or that. But here it's his house, and he sees that. And it's his kids, and he wants to do things for them. His mother, I think, was the one who taught them all that, and he's still that way. Some of the guys laugh at the ones who help their wives around the house, even cooking and all. . . . Some of them call them names you wouldn't want to hear, but he don't care, and they don't call any names like that at him. He says, 'Let them laugh. That's their problem.'"

Other stresses were imposed on the mining families in addition to those arising from the miners' working conditions. The family income was rarely secure over long periods of time, and the threat of unemployment from strikes, layoffs, and shutdowns was never far away. Any of these events meant that the family would lose its income for a period ranging from a few days to many months. Even when the economy was strong and the mines had been working hard, fluctuations in the market price of coal, disagreements between the union and the company, or just temporary vacation times could put the miners out of work. Moreover, it was commonly known that the number of accidents was likely to increase when the miners returned to work after a period of unemployment, and this added to the families' concerns.

Many families tried to plan ahead for these circumstances by saving money, paying bills ahead when possible, purchasing or preserving extra food and household supplies, or having a secondary source of income or food such as a small farm. Their methods of preparing for strikes, layoffs, and shutdowns were generally quite efficient. However, even the most effective preparation could provide no more than temporary help when the mines were closed down for more than a few weeks.

Strikes were the most frequent causes of income loss and, because the cause of a strike might be questionable, sometimes created strains within the family. Some strikes took place to call attention to poor conditions in the mine where the miners were working, or to protest some unfair treatment of miners either in the home mines or mines in other areas. In these cases, the temporary loss of income might mean that better working conditions in the mine or better treatment would be gained after the strike was settled. There was little disagreement within the families when some improvement in working conditions might be made, and some of the miners' wives joined in the strikers' demonstrations or became activists in other ways (Maggard 1990a; Scott 1988).

However, strikes were occasionally called to support demands in the home mine that were considered to be less important or to support miners who were striking in other mines for less important reasons. Some of the women saw the loss of income caused by these strikes as a loss with no compensation or a loss for no useful reason. When such strikes had occurred in the past, there had been disagreements between the women and their husbands over the miners' participation. If the strike continued and the women felt it necessary to find outside employment to supplement the small strike funds, disagreements sometimes grew heated.

Cora, Mary, and Flo discussed their feelings about the different causes of strikes and agreed, "Sometimes you just feel the only thing they can do is go out. . . . Something might have gotten so bad that they [the miners] can't go on. The companies don't listen to anything else sometimes, and, you know, they don't care. . . . They just plain don't care about what happens to the ones that work down there. You have to get their attention somehow, and money is what they listen to. When it's like that, then you don't mind going without. You go through what you have, and then you have to find some money to come in from somewhere and usually that means going out and working. And you don't mind that. It's to make things better.

"But sometimes they go out for nothing . . . some little thing that's not important. That's when it gets you. One time they went out because they wanted better showers. One time they all walked out because one pump didn't get fixed fast enough . . . one pump. Well, I get annoyed, and he gets annoyed at me, and then we argue about it. . . . He says I don't understand, and maybe I don't. But . . . it's our living that suffers, our savings that get spent, and sometimes I just get mad about it. When it's a good cause, I help. I've carried a sign, and stood out in the street in front of the company office in the rain, and did all my own work, and worked at the discount store to help with the money. I don't feel like doing that when it's some little thing."

When a strike continued longer than a few weeks, family resources were depleted, and reserves were likely to disappear completely. Because there were few other sources of employment for the miners, the family might become dependent on union strike funds and the income the miner's wife could earn. When strike funds were gone, families were completely dependent on the women's earnings. If these were too small to carry the family's expenses and no other jobs were available for anyone in the family, help from family, friends, church and charity funds, government, and other sources became the only means of surviving. Over the years destitution was occasionally the consequence of long-drawn-out strikes; the living conditions of mining families during such strikes were at bare subsistence levels (Caudill 1973; Corbin 1981; Maggard 1990a, 1990b; Naughton 1988; Walker 1932).

Like many other Appalachian women with relatively poor educational backgrounds and the need to work (Maggard 1990a, 1990b), the oldest women in the group had worked at all of the part-time and full-time jobs available in the area for women with no professional or technical training. Mary said, "I've done just about everything. I've worked in a store, cleaned houses, delivered papers, worked in a restaurant, worked in an office doing filing and things like that. I've helped farm, worked in a factory. You name it. If you can do it around here, I've probably done it sometime or other."

Helen also had taken many jobs, usually because her husband was out on strike. "I just hated strikes. We both hated strikes. You never got caught up, got ahead. . . . You just didn't get anywhere no matter where you found some job to do. He'd come home with this look on his face like it was down on the floor, and I'd know. Sometimes you got money from the union, and sometimes there wasn't any. I've scrubbed floors, waited tables, worked for a church once doing cleaning, even worked on a farm. You've got to make the effort. You can't just sit there. There's no money coming in, but the kids have got to go to school, and they've go to have lunches to take and shoes to wear. There's just no feeling like knowing you've got nothing coming in and a family to take care of. I've seen him cry about it and I've cried too.

"People don't know, if they never had to go through it. You've got kids to feed and . . . I'll tell you . . . sometimes meals were a problem. There were times when we'd eat beans until the kids wouldn't eat no more, and a couple times we got to where we had to get help from someplace just to get anything to eat. The time I worked in a church, there wasn't no work around here for anyone. . . . We got down to where I didn't know what we was going to eat in a couple days. I went to the preacher and asked, 'What are we going to do?' He said, 'You can come and work here.' . . . It didn't pay much at all, but it was something coming in. He gave us some canned things to help get us through, and it's not a feeling you want, to know you're living off charity. Then they [the church] decided they liked having the church kept so good, and they paid more, and I kept on working there for four years."

Some of the older women had worked part time during particular seasons as well as during strikes. Mary worked during strikes and also every summer to earn extra money for her children's school clothing and supplies. She remembered how she felt as a young girl when she realized that she would be unable to finish school because her family could not continue to provide schoolbooks, clothing, and shoes. She also remembered that her determination that her children would go all the way through school was a major part of her motivation to work through the summers and, during the other seasons, often on weekends as well.

"Sometimes it seemed like I worked all the time. Strikes was the worst because then there was only me to bring in money. . . . You didn't get anything from anywhere else like you do now. But in the summers, I got up early, got things done, then went and worked in [a grocery store] all day. I'd come home, get supper, then take us all with me to the park that was there at the time and work at the concession stand there. When the oldest was real young, just a baby, I clerked in another store. Had to walk back and forth. I'd pick up the baby, carry her down the hill to the settlement house, and walk to work. After work, I'd walk back to the settlement house, pick her up, and carry her up the hill. It made things easier for us all. . . . We wouldn't have had anything otherwise when he was on strike.

"When we wasn't on strike, I bought things for the children—books, or an extra jacket or pair of shoes, or something they wanted. My girl always liked hair ribbons, and if I could buy her one, it made me feel good. The mine paid better than anyplace else, but it wasn't enough to pay for all that a family needs. There's always something that you need, and maybe you can get along without it, but it makes your family life happier sometimes if you can get extra things. But there were years and years when the work wasn't steady, when they went out sometimes for months, and then you didn't always know where the food was coming from. If I was working, there was always that to keep us."

During strikes or layoffs, the need for an income usually acted to reduce any feelings of family discontent over changes or disruptions in home routines caused by the homemaker's absence. Even though most of the husbands preferred that their wives be full-time homemakers, they were thankful that the women could find jobs during difficult times. Some husbands helped with housework or other chores when the women were working through a strike or layoff, although most men did not. When the women no longer obviously needed to work outside the home but wished to continue to work, tensions sometimes arose between husband and wife. If the women enjoyed their outside work, these tensions could become difficult to resolve.

Many of the older women and some of the younger women continued to work after strikes or layoffs ended, even though their husbands had returned to full-time employment. At the time of our conversations, the length of time that employment continued subsequent to a strike or layoff ranged across the group from less than a year to continuous employment. In each case, however, the women, their husbands, and sometimes their children had to make adjustments that occasionally were difficult. None of the families appeared to have been spared the need to realign their thoughts and feelings about "the woman of the family" working.

Rose recalled, "Once I got started, I wanted to do it. I liked it, and it meant more money coming in, and that was nice. He never liked it, never wanted me to work outside the house. He said he wasn't going to tell me I couldn't do it, because he knew that would just make me mad. But the day I quit work, he was so glad. We hardly got to have any time together when I was working. We just passed each other and maybe talked for a few minutes and that was that. If he worked nights, then we'd have some time together after dinner, but there was never enough time to really sit down and talk about things like we liked to. Even when he worked days, our schedules didn't go together very well. They was just enough off that we didn't get much time together, and it wasn't at the right time.

"Then there'd be things he'd have to do at home, and he didn't much like to do them. He did them, he wanted to help me, he said he did, and I believed him. We've always helped each other. But he didn't really like doing it, and sometimes I didn't like the way he did it. Then I'd do it over and he wouldn't like that. It got so I didn't know what to do—to do things over and him be cross or not do it and I'd be cross. Finally, after a couple years, all the fuss at home just got to the point where I thought I was just making things worse for myself. I just got tired of it and told them I was quitting."

The younger women's experiences with working outside the home did not differ greatly from those of the older women, although the younger women's attitudes about working were more varied than those of the older women. The younger women had held fewer jobs than the older women because the period of time in their marriages in which it had been necessary for them to find jobs had been fewer. The type of work found by the younger women had also been less diverse although, like the older women, they had been employed at many different types of jobs.

About half of the younger women believed that women should be free to have a career outside the home regardless of whether or not it was financially necessary. Some of the more outspoken younger women believed that any adjustments that would have to be made at home if a woman chose to work would have to be seen as being as necessary as those made for a husband's employment. Their view was, as Paula said, "Compromise is something that has to be to both of us [wives and husbands]." Despite these attitudes, however, few saw themselves as free to "do their thing" until their children were older. When that day came, they intended to work at outside occupations of their choice if possible. Those who enjoyed working before their marriages and during their early years of marriage, in particular, looked forward to working again.

Lynn said, "We've talked about my working when the children are older, and that's what I want to do. It'll get my mind off of him down there and give me a chance to be with other people more. I worked in an office before I got pregnant, and I really liked it. The only time I work anywhere now is if he's on strike and they stay out . . . but you can't really get a really good job when you only work when there's a strike. It eats up your savings really fast. . . . You can't really get ahead enough to live on for very long . . . a couple of weeks, maybe a month, and then you've got only something for maybe emergencies and maybe not even that. I worry about it, about the money going so fast and maybe not being able to pay for something that you have to have. . . . You never know when you'll need money for some emergency.

"If I have a regular job, we'd have more ahead, and working will give me something of my own to think about. I'm not just here for other people. I'm here for me too. I'm important too, and I want to feel like there's this job that I do that's all mine. He understands even if he don't like it when I talk about going to work . . . but he feels the same way about his job. He's said at night, 'Look there. See all them lights out there. . . . None of them would be there if we wasn't mining coal. . . . I helped to put them lights there.' That's the way I used to feel about my job. . . even if it was only secretarial work. It accomplished something that meant something. Here I look around and it's not that I haven't accomplished something, but . . . I want something of my own. And I think, 'What if something does happen to him? What have I got then? . . . How would I take care of us?'"

Ginny and Sharon agreed with Lynn's comments that working outside the home brought satisfactions that could not easily be found at home. Sharon said, "I want to work when they're [the children] older because it gets me out, puts me with other people. It's not really the money even if that helps. It's really being out every day with other adults . . . having some place where there's just you and the other people. . . . It's hard to explain, but being at home all the time is like being kept away from people. I like being here. I like taking care of him and the baby and the house, but I want there to be more than that to my life."

While some younger women, like Lynn, felt that being employed outside the home could be another form of insurance against the kind of loss they would experience if their husbands died in the mines, most did not want to talk about work in that context. They found it very difficult to discuss working as a possible preparation for widowhood, just as they had found it difficult to discuss the dangers that threatened their husbands in the mines. The threat of death in the mines was such an immediate threat that conversations about widowhood were not held frequently or sustained for very long.

When they married, all of the women knew there was a higher than average likelihood of becoming a widow while they were still young or middle aged and had small children at home. Regardless of how optimistic they wished to be when they were first married, hearing and talking about fatal and near-fatal accidents in the mines made them aware of their vulnerability. Their parents had tried to plan for this likelihood by building financial security in property or insurance, and the women and their husbands had done the same. Most, for example, owned their own homes, had purchased some form of life insurance, and tried to build up savings accounts. Some tried to find feelings of security in the knowledge that parents or other relatives would help them through (Althouse 1974).

For women with small children, however, the modest levels of financial security they had been able to achieve did not greatly alleviate the stress of knowing that losing their husbands would leave them alone and responsible for supporting their families. They were familiar with the potential sources of money that would be available to them if something happened to their husbands, and they were not reassured about the adequacy of these funds. For some women, even discussions of the possibility of widowhood created additional stress when their concerns were turned aside by their husbands' reluctance to think about dying in the mines.

Carrie and Louise were two of the women whose worries about the consequences of losing their husbands in the mines had become particularly disturbing because their husbands had difficulty in discussing the issues that were involved. Carrie had three children still at home. She said her husband believed they were adequately covered by insurance, but she had never been able to persuade her husband to discuss her concerns about the kind of life she would be able to make for herself and her children if he were to die in the mine. His seemingly casual acceptance of such a fate disturbed her, and her failure to engage him in planning for the future made her irritated.

"I have a hard time with this. Every time, he just laughs and says, 'If I die today, you'll have someone else tomorrow.' Things like that really bother me, but we can't talk about it. . . . If I push him to talk about what would I do, he gets mad. He won't even let me talk about it if I'm talking about someone else. . . . He says I shouldn't think about it, but I do think about it. It comes up because there are things that bring it up. And when there's an accident, even a little thing, how can you not think about it? I think, 'What would happen to me? Here I am with three kids. What would I do?' All he ever says is, 'There's insurance, you'd get along somehow.'"

For Louise, the conflicts between her attitudes and those of her husband came from his arguments that working in the mines was not very dangerous. She said, 'He says we got all the insurance we need, and the union would help us too. Then he says, 'Stop worrying,' because they try to make things safe at his mine. He says he feels he is safe, and he says, 'If I feel safe, you don't need to worry.' But I know there are a lot of things he doesn't tell me, because he doesn't want me to worry, and then I just worry more because I don't know what he's not telling me. I have a neighbor who's a widow, and her husband died in the same mine doing the same job that he does. His wife [the neighbor's wife] tried to believe he was safe too. . . . I know he teased her about her worrying about him. I want to believe that it is safe but then . . . I know they can't prevent some things from happening no matter how safe they say it is. I watched her when he died, and I know what she went through. And I watch her now and wonder whether it'll happen to me and how it would be for me."

For some women, thoughts of widowhood were too fright-ening to entertain, and they pushed the thoughts away when they occurred. Some said, as Ginny did, "I can't think about it at all. . . . I know we have insurance but that isn't what bothers me. It's what might happen to him . . . and then to me. I just can't think about it. I don't want to know about acci-dents. I don't want to hear him talk about it. He says, 'If it's going to happen, it's going to happen' . . . but I don't want to hear about that. . . . I really get mad when he talks like that. He's just so carefree and casual about it like it wasn't going to happen to him, and I just can't deal with that. I know I should know all about our insurance and all about the health plan, all that . . . but I just can't deal with it, because I get mad at him . . . at his attitude."

The difficulties of life for widows in the coal communities included more than just financial problems, and some of the noneconomic problems were particularly painful for the several women who were or had been widows. Their initial financial difficulties were often serious and immediate even though the family might have had adequate life insurance. Money from insurance companies, union benefits, and other sources of funds usually did not arrive quickly enough to prevent problems with such living expenses as house or car payments and bills for food, utilities, and so on. At first, friends, neighbors, church members, families, and occasionally even company officials would offer help of various kinds to sustain the family. As time went on, the widow's family might continue to offer help, but others who had offered help returned to their family and work concerns.

The preference among mining families for socializing primarily with other mining families (Althouse 1974) often meant that the loss of a husband removed the miner's widow from her primary social group of married couples. If she had continued in this social group, her presence would have been a constant reminder of the likelihood of death. Not only would she have been a reminder of what could happen to her friends' husbands but the conversation among the women in the group would have to have changed to reflect the widow's new situation. The women's daily activities revolved around the miners' working schedules and the tasks that were necessary to maintain family equilibrium in the context of their work; a widow no longer had the same concerns or restraints as her former friends.

A widow's continued presence in the social group would also be awkward because she was now a single woman. If she was attractive, she might constitute a threat to the other women's marriages. Even her needs might be perceived as a threat by other women in the group if their husbands provided help or emotional support to her. The transition from social group member to former member was a slow and difficult process. A major part of the widow's adjustment was the redefinition of her daily life to accommodate to these multiple losses.

At the time we talked, Amy had been a widow for five years. She thought her adjustment had been very slow and that she would not have made it without the continuing support of her parents, aunts, and uncles. "I couldn't even talk about it . . . couldn't say the word 'dead,' never used the word 'widow.' I just couldn't accept it. I kept his clothes in the closet, toothbrush on the holder, even kept his shoes under the bed. I believed he wasn't dead. I got up every day thinking about what I'd put in his lunch bucket. I don't know how they put up with me for those couple years. But then one day they said, 'It's time now you straighten up. . . . We all miss him. . . . Think about your children. . . . Put his things away. . . . You've got a life to live.'"

Of her former friends, Amy said, "They was helpful at first. . . . They would have done anything for me they could, but they have families to take care of and worries of their own. After things settled down, I saw I wasn't really a part of their life anymore. It wasn't anything big you know, but after a while we just didn't talk as much on the phone. And one day when I went to a school activity, I saw they [her friends] came in together. They didn't ask me to go along with them. . . . It was like there was something between us. It wasn't that they were unfriendly or anything like that, but I just wasn't a part of them anymore. It really came to me how much things had changed.

"There were others that died when he died, and I saw that after a while their wives were just off on their own. It wasn't just me. It was just what happened. A couple of the young ones started living with men. . . . I can't blame them. You got to get along somehow. And the one older woman had a man as a boarder, and after a year they got married. But other women talked about all of them. Everyone knew what was going on. Even the pastor wasn't forgiving . . . but I thought, 'He doesn't know how hard it is to get along by yourself.' Most of them still live here. A couple got married again, and the rest are like me. And, well, you have to get on with living. . . . I'm only just recently thinking about what I want for myself. . . . Some ways it still seems . . . new."

Flo was in her early twenties when her first husband died in the mines. "I was a little, you know, crazy. . . . I'd go to work or I'd skip it and stay home and cry. . . . I didn't want to stay home, but I didn't want to be with other people. I just wanted him back. I'd go out, maybe to the store or just to walk around the stores or to my mother's house, and then I'd come back before I got there. I'd stay in the house and not even answer the phone. I wanted someone to talk to, and I'd get mad if someone called to talk to me. I was hateful to everyone. I blamed him. I blamed God. I blamed the company. I just couldn't face it.

"Some of his friends would stop to see how I was. And I knew their wives didn't like it. They [the wives] got so they didn't like me. . . . I knew what they thought. . . . They didn't want their men stopping to see me, but his friends stopped to see if there was anything they could do. We didn't really have anybody else. My family was all. We didn't run around much with other people, but he had friends in the mine where I didn't have any. Well, I had some, but they were his friends' wives, and I only knew the wives because of him. That's the way it is with a lot of miners' wives. . . . You got the friends you have because the men work together."

The widows's adjustment problems were often compounded by the need to find work to add income to the funds received from insurance benefits and social security. Finding such employment was difficult in a local economy where mining or mining-related jobs were likely to be the only high-wage jobs available. Older women, in particular, were handicapped in the job search. They had few marketable job skills, because they were likely to have been employed only part time or for short periods of time in service-level jobs at low wages. In contrast, younger women were likely to have worked longer prior to and after marriage and to have been employed at lower-level white-collar jobs. In mining communities, however, such differences in marketable skills were often leveled out by the small number of jobs available.

After their husbands died, Flo and Amy eventually had to find work to supplement their incomes. They worked as waitresses, store clerks, and nurses' aides and doing house cleaning. Eventually, Flo married again although she continued to work outside the home and hoped to become self-employed in the future. Amy had worked as a clerical worker early in her marriage, but after her husband died, she was unable to find any work other than low-wage service jobs. Amy and several other mining widows she knew constantly experienced the frustration of not having quite enough money to go around.

Amy said she often juggled thoughts of wanting a better job, being a full-time homemaker again, and the yearly increases in the cost of food, clothing, medical care, home maintenance, transportation, insurance, and utilities. She would like to have a better education for herself and said she thought about the different ways of financing school, but none seemed possible in her circumstances. She said she and her friends felt they could get their children off to an adequate start in life, but when they thought about their own futures, they were not optimistic.

FIVE

Coping:
Work, Faith, and Denial

The daily lives of the miners' wives were shaped by a constellation of social, economic, and physical conditions with clear potential for creating high levels of stress. For example, corporate economic interests were best served by having workers work around the clock, and economic considerations were often the cause of layoffs and shutdowns. The consequences for mining families were the frustrating family and personal problems that arose from the rotating work shifts and threats to family income. Social tradition, however, was responsible for the notion that the miners' wives should take on the burden of responsibility for creating a stress-free home for their husbands. Moreover, tradition also decreed that, when necessary, the women should bear the additional tensions and physical strains of being wage earner–homemakers.

The physical conditions in which mining was carried out created the dangers of the work and the pervasive anxiety-creating awareness that death or serious injury could disrupt the lives of the wives at any time. Moreover, for some women, contradictions between older and newer social ideas about women's place in the home and marriage generated stressful inner conflicts. Younger women, in particular, made it clear that these conflicts could be traced directly to the old and usually unvoiced assumption that a woman's personal needs and wishes would be secondary to her husband's for as many years as he was able, or chose, to go under the mountain and bring out coal.

How did they cope with this combination of pressures and how well did their coping methods work to relieve the inner strain? Some studies of working-class families who were experiencing social and economic stressors such as frequent unemployment and adverse working conditions have shown that, if the coping strategies they employed were effective, the stresses and strains they experienced were reduced to a bearable level. That is, effective coping strategies were related to tolerable levels of psychological distress. On the other hand, if coping strategies were ineffective, each morning began a new battle to survive the day despite tension, anxiety, depression, and hopelessness (Pearlin and Lieberman 1978; Pearlin and Schooler 1978; Pearlin 1980).

The most effective methods of coping with stress and strain were found to be those aimed at changing or eliminating the source of the stress (the stressor) or removing individuals from the stressful circumstances. A variety of other, less effective, methods were aimed at influencing people's perceptions of the stressors; that is, these methods influenced what people thought about the stressors (Pearlin 1980). For the miners' wives, the most effective coping methods would have been elimination or alteration of the conditions under which their husbands worked. The less effective methods of coping required the women to somehow change their perceptions of the stressors and the threats they imposed.

It was clear that, given the conditions of mining, some direct coping strategies could not possibly be used; that is, the women could not change the geological nature of the coal seams or the hazards inherent in the basic processes of mining. The coal seams their husbands worked were buried deep underground, and shafts had to be sunk vertically or tunnels opened diagonally hundreds of feet into the mountains to reach them. Explosives, machinery, and men had to be used to break the embedded coal away from its surrounding rock, and the coal had to be conveyed quickly to the outside world by some method. Each mechanical process involved in production of coal added to the overall dangers of the occupation.

Other stressors involved in mining were also relatively unchangeable given the prevailing economic structures and the attitudes of the coal companies. The companies, for example, might have imposed fewer risks on miners if they had employed the newest mining techniques, but then as now concerns about profits rather than about the welfare of the workers who produced the coal determined the methods of mining. Other useful changes would also have had detrimental effects on profit-making. For example, eliminating rotating shifts was believed to reduce production and therefore profits. Stabilizing coal production to prevent shutdowns and layoffs was also believed to reduce production and profits, and strikes were blamed on workers, not companies.

Another direct coping strategy was available in theory: people could remove themselves from the stressful circumstances; that is, the mining families could move to other locations where other occupational opportunities might be found. However, the bonds of attachment to home and kin among the families were generations deep and so strong that few chose to live away from kin. Moreover, earning a living in a way that few others would choose had become an emotional bond tying people to the land and the mines. The rigors of mining and the problems they caused for mining families were accepted as the daily conditions of life, and for many enduring and surviving these conditions became a source of pride.

Given these circumstances, we were not surprised to learn in our conversations that direct coping strategies were not likely to be employed by the miners' wives or in mining families in general. The women used methods aimed at reducing the stress of worry indirectly by influencing their perceptions of, and reactions to, the causes of stress in their lives. Many of the women used work as a way of combating stress, and many also used rationalizations of various kinds. Some relied heavily on denial and some on their faith in God's will. Regardless of the method they chose, however, all but one or two said they were seldom able to find more than temporary relief from worry.

Most of the older women and some younger women believed that work was the most effective way to cope with worry, depression, and anxiety. Although they said they did not rely on one coping strategy alone to relieve stress, they felt that work occupied the mind and temporarily displaced other concerns more effectively than other ways of coping. Older women, in particular, preferred work as a way of keeping worry out of mind. Mary looked back over the more than forty years she had been a miner's wife and said, "You've got to keep as busy as you can. You just can't sit there and do nothing with all that on your mind. You've got to make an effort to get up and work and keep going. You might not want to, and it might seem like it takes all you can do to get up and do something, but you've go to do something."

Other women agreed, and the older women pointed out that coping with worry sometimes seemed easiest in the years when they were the busiest. The years when their children were growing up had been so busy with child rearing, homemaking tasks, and periodic outside employment that, in comparison to later years, the almost constant hard work had relieved much of the surface burden of worry. They said, "You got to pay attention to all that has to be done at home, and then, if you're working somewhere, you've got to somehow fit all that in. There wasn't hardly a day that wasn't busy from the minute you got up to the time you went to bed. You'd worry underneath. . . . That was always there, but keeping busy with the children and dusting and sweeping and cooking and all that took some of the worries off your mind in the daytime."

Helen recalled, "At first I didn't have enough to keep me busy. . . . Married women didn't work unless they had to then, and he didn't want me to work, so I'd polish and clean and wash and iron and then I did it again. That sounds so crazy, but I really would do it over again. Then when my girl was born and then my boy came along, I had plenty to do, but that's what I wanted—it was working kept me from worrying as much. Sometimes I cried, and if they saw me, they cried right along with me because we didn't know if their daddy was coming home. . . . But I didn't want them to worry, so I'd get busy and we'd do things together. We'd color or sew or sing songs or I'd teach them Bible stories sometimes the whole evening when he worked nights. Now my daughter has her own, and she does the same thing. . . . She says it just seems natural."

Some women found that creative work or an outside occupation allowed them to turn their minds to other considerations. Needle craft, pottery, teaching music or crafts, working at a part-time or full-time job, or volunteer work for their church had become coping strategies for a few women. Working with others in useful tasks, the application of thought and effort, and the hours invested in these activities had given respite to some from thinking about conditions they could not change.

Cora related her experiences as she had looked for and finally found activities to occupy her time. "When the children got to where they didn't need me so much, then it got to be a problem. . . . It was kind of gradual, but I tried a lot of things to fill up my time and keep it out of my mind . . . keep from thinking about him and what this life is like for him and me, mostly just worrying. I just looked for anything, anything to keep busy. . . . I picked at needle craft but that didn't really help. . . . I tried reading and that wasn't it either. . . . I worked off and on when we had to, of course, but I didn't really want to do that. Then I started doing volunteer work, and now I've done that for years. . . . I could have a full-time volunteer job. There's such a need. It helps me feel better to know I can help someone . . . not just think of my own worries all the time. . . . It makes me know there's others got it a lot worse than I've got. It sounds awful, I guess, to say it. But when I can help someone else who's worse off, then I know I've done something."

While work was a preferred method of coping with worry for many women, rationalization either alone or in combination with work was the preferred method for others. The women who felt that rationalization helped them cope with stress believed that comparing their day-to-day situations to the experiences of other women or to their own worse experiences placed current worries in a less disturbing context. Women whose parents and grandparents had been miners also felt that some comparisons, such as comparing mining in the past with mining in the present, served as reminders that mining families were considerably better off than they had been in earlier years. In comparison, contemporary worries should have been lighter.

Beth's father had been a miner for more than twenty years, and she reflected, "We should be glad that things are a lot better than they used to be. When I was a child, my dad worked with a pick and shovel. They used horses then, things was really bad for the miners. I remember how he'd come home with his hands hurt, his back. One time he got his chest almost crushed. It's better now—there's better equipment, and they've got safety equipment. . . . A lot of them don't use it but it's there. I think of my mother, and I realize how much better I have it and how much better it is all around for us . . . more money, more safety equipment. They know more about things like that. When I feel bad, I try and remember that we're lucky compared to then."

Carrie lived in a neighborhood where most of her neighbors were mining families. She felt she was fortunate, because her husband had never been injured seriously even though some of the neighbor men had been seriously injured at one time or another and several miners' widows lived near her. "I guess I do worry a lot. But when it gets really hard . . . if he's late coming home or if it all just builds up on me, I tell myself I've got it easier than some I know. I hear how hard it can be. We all talk about it when we get together. I know how hard it was for [my neighbor] when her husband was out for over a month, and they didn't know at first if he'd ever go back. His back was so bad. I know how she worried.

"He tells me he's got it easier than some too, that his job's nothing compared to what some do. . . . And he tells me about this one or that one that works up at the face or has to work with all the electrical cables and things. He says he feels lucky he only has to deal with machinery, and he tries to make it seem not so dangerous, so I won't worry. I tell myself to think how hard it is for the ones whose husbands got killed. . . . My worries are nothing compared to what they have to do to get along. I've got my husband. That's the most important thing. And they've lost everything."

Combining rationalization and working was a strategy often called upon in coping with situations such as strikes and layoffs. Working outside the home eased the financial strain while rationalization allowed the necessity of taking on extra work to be seen as potentially beneficial in the future. Paula, one of the younger women, explained, "You really have to have the money. . . . You can just wipe out your savings in just a few weeks, so you have to get out and do something. There's a lot of strain for me because I just can't see what's going to happen to us. . . . Is this going to last for a week? a month? How long are we going to be out of work? It's a scary thing when you see the money going out every week and you're not doing anything.

"Working helps with the money, and then it's good because it gets you out of the house and away from him, and he knows you can help. . . . It isn't just all on him. It gets you to the place where you can begin to think, 'Hey, I can do something too . . . I'm a worker too. And then I begin to feel like it shows them [the coal company] you just won't take everything they want to shove down your throat. I think about what I can do and how much better off we are because I can help take care of us, and it does help some with worrying. I'd rather be at home, but bringing home a paycheck makes me feel better about taking care of anything that might happen. I don't want to do it, but it makes a difference in how I feel."

The wives coped with stress by using rationalizations to modify their perceptions, not only in relation to specific stressors such as strikes or the dangers of mining but also when thinking and talking about general conditions. Ginny said, for example, "When I read in the paper about something that happens it reminds me that everyone's got something about their life that can be bad even if you work in an office or clerk in a store. You can get sick or lose your job or your house could burn down or you could lose your children, and it isn't just working in a mine that can make life hard, you know. Anyone's life can be hard, not just a miner's."

Paula agreed with Ginny's assessment and said, "He's got about the worst job in the world, but we've got other things, and sometimes just thinking about those other things is the best thing I can do to make myself feel better. There's some in [a nearby town] who've lost their homes and never got them back. There's a family right down here [down the street], and their little girl died of leukemia. And a family right across from us, and their boy got killed in a car accident. Mine are running around here happy and healthy, so there's a lot who have it worse than we do. It doesn't make his job any different to think about what you have and how bad it can be for other people, but you have to try to see things in your life compared to what it's like for other people."

Nearly all of the women believed that denial was the least effective coping strategy, yet they felt it did play a part in reducing their anxiety. A few called upon denial combined with working and rationalization to alleviate tensions, while others believed that denial alone was the most useful way to cope with some specific situations. They made it clear that suppressing thoughts or words about the dangers their husbands faced seemed to be the only way for them to cope day by day. Their lives seemed simpler if they could avoid talking or thinking or even hearing about their husbands' working conditions.

Laura believed that working was the best way for her to control her stress, but she also believed she coped better with some circumstances by denying them. "Mining's just like that. . . . It's dangerous. It always will be. If you want coal you're going to work underground . . . at least here anyway, and there's nothing I can do about it. He wants to be a miner, always has. . . . There's nothing I can do about that. . . . It's his choice. You couldn't get him to move away and do anything else. The company only cares about money. . . . I can't change that either . . . so I don't think about it. I don't talk about it. I push it out of my mind. If I don't, it'd get to me. It can just take over. It can make you sick."

Ginny agreed, "There are some things you just can't talk about because you can't make it any different. I don't think you can ever . . . ever . . . really deal with most of them so I avoid them. If I can't make it any different, then I don't want to deal with it. I have a friend who even reads about the geology here [in the coal mountains]. I don't want to know that. I don't want to think about things I can't do anything about. . . . I have enough to worry about, you know—whether he's coming back, whether he'll have a job next week. I can only deal with so much and stay balanced.

"There's lots of dangerous jobs. If he was driving a truck, that'd be just as dangerous. . . . Accidents can happen anywhere. . . . You can work in a store and get killed or hurt in an accident. You can live all your life and then get killed on your way home. If I thought about all that, I'd never be able to get through the day. Sometimes I get so depressed, I just have to make myself remember that he could be doing something else and get hurt. . . . I have to put it out of my mind. I try and think of something happy. I just have to tell myself it won't happen to him, tell myself he's going to be all right. . . . We're going to get through the bad times."

Karen reflected on the changes in her coping strategies that have occurred over time and compared her present way of coping with her earlier ways. "I've seen what it's like down there. I went through because I had to know and I wanted to know. Then I used to get all torn up about it, but that makes everything worse. I'd be so cranky and irritable nobody could stand to be around me. If he was late, even a little, I'd be standing at the window looking for him. I waited up for him every night. . . . I started worrying about him before he even got there. Everything bothered me. . . . I worried about money, about him, about what I'd do if something happened to him, just everything. I even worried about the kids when nothing was wrong. I just had to stop. I was making myself sick.

"I had to force myself to think more positively about it. I had to tell myself nothing's going to happen to him. He isn't going to end up killed. I had to remind myself he makes real good money. Men do get hurt but he's careful. He's good at his job, and it's not worse than some other jobs can be. I just don't think about what could happen. . . . You can call it avoidance but it's the only way I can get along. I don't listen to talk about accidents. I don't want to know when something goes wrong. I don't read about it. I don't want to hear his friends talk about it. . . . I can't handle it, so I don't think about it."

In addition to relying on work, rationalization, and denial, almost all of the older women and some of the younger women held deep and strong religious beliefs, a source of comfort that was common in other mining areas as well (Scott

1988). For some, their faith in God had become their primary coping method. Two of the women had been reborn in the Christian faith and believed they had found some relief from worry, anxiety, and depression in their spiritual rebirth. Other women believed their religious faith had begun to grow strong in their childhood or adolescence and had never failed to provide a measure of comfort. Older women, in particular, recalled earlier days when desperate need and prayer had been followed by help that had come from the church, its ministers, or members. Those with strongest beliefs said they had been shown, sometimes repeatedly, that God would take care of His children.

Some of the women who believed that their religious faith was important in their lives, but not necessarily a constant primary influence, felt uncertainty about the role of their faith in coping with stress. Sharon and Carol, for example, had both expressed some hesitation about whether or not they could rely on their faith in God as a way of relieving anxiety. They both believed themselves to be Christians, and both believed in God and in God's will as the determining factor in people's lives. However, Carol said, "I don't know. It seems like you ought to be able to just say God will take care of him and us and not worry, but I can't. I guess I'm not sure. I believe in God's will, and I believe He'll take care of us, but that doesn't make me feel any better."

Similar uncertainty was expressed by a few other women who talked about the difficulty of believing that God would or could be the determining factor in both overall and specific life events. Although they considered themselves believers in the Christian faith, they felt that God's words only provided guidelines for people to follow throughout their lives. The actual events that occurred in people's lives were determined by earthly rather than spiritual causes whether or not a person chose to follow these teachings. Laura said, "What causes things to happen is people. Someone isn't careful or they're tired or in a hurry. . . . That's when accidents happen. I don't think God has anything to do with it. Maybe He knows when someone's going to die, but I don't think He makes it happen . . . or not happen."

A few women relied on their religious faith as a primary means of coping with stress. Their reliance was based upon their belief that the world, its people, and events were all parts of a higher plan. Within this belief system, coping required only that individuals acknowledge that their power to control their lives was limited and accept that they would be cared for according to God's plan. The women who believed most strongly in this view had experienced a "born again" renewal of their faith, although not all of those who relied primarily on faith as a coping method had been reborn.

Flo said her emotional reactions to the conditions of her life had only troubled her "severely" when she forgot that help for all problems was immediately available through faith. A year or so after her husband was killed in the mine, she experienced a rebirth in her faith, and she recalled it as intensely moving and unforgettable. Before that time she had, she said, "never thought much of church. I wasn't the church type. I liked dancing and drinking. We both did. After he was killed, my brother kept after me and after me to go with him to church, and one night I did—more to keep him quiet than anything else. When the preacher asked for people to come down, I just rose up and went down that aisle like I was floating. . . . I don't think my feet were touching the floor. I found God. I found where I belonged. And I can tell you that when I say 'floated,' I never felt anything like that before.

"I believe in the Bible, and I believe all the answers are in there. When I get to worrying so much I can't take it, I can open it up and take my finger and drop it on a page, and it seems like it always falls on something that answers my problems. When things start to bother me, when I get to worrying, it helps to know I can go there and find an answer. I don't just read page after page. I jump . . . like maybe halfway back or anyplace at all, and it seems like no matter what's on my mind, God knows what's there . . . and it just comes out . . . right there in the Bible. It has helped me keep from worrying so much. . . . I know the Lord has a plan for me. I'm part of it. . . . We all are. . . . And it helps to know that."

There was general agreement among the women that the Bible could help by providing advice, direction, or consolation during times of stress. Most, however, relied less on reading the Bible or pinpointing a helpful biblical statement than on prayer or reflection on the existence of a higher plan for all people. Many both older and younger believed as Rose did that "prayer is a big help when you feel bad. . . . If you just take a deep breath and sit back and think about the fact that your life is just one part . . . and pray . . . you feel better. If it's His will that you lose your husband or a child or anybody, then it's the way it's going to be and nothing you can do will change it. You don't have to worry. . . . You do what you can do and that's what's important, that you *do* what you can but the rest is in His hands. It might not seem right, you might not understand it, but there's nothing you can do to change it."

Amy reflected on her rejection of her religious faith during the time immediately following her husband's death, and her return to its comfort later. "We usually went to church even when it meant me going by myself, and we took the children to Sunday School, and my girl was in the choir. After he got killed, I was just so hateful. . . . I hated everyone. I hated the company, I hated the other ones with him that didn't get killed, and I hated God for taking my husband. I didn't want to talk to the preacher or to anyone from there, and after a while they stopped coming here, and I was glad. I stopped going to church for a long time. I didn't want to believe that God would let my husband die like that. I felt, 'If God loved us like the church says then why would He take my husband?'

"One day the preacher started coming around again, and he kept talking to me about how God has a plan for all of us in everything that happens. I didn't want to see him. The first time he come up, I didn't let him in, pretended I wasn't here. But he kept on coming up to see me, and one Sunday I went to church. Then I started going again now and then, and I came to believe like he said, 'God has a reason for everything that happens.' I don't understand it. Here I am and my husband is dead. But I stopped hating God, and I think I accept it now . . . and accepting it helped me to get better. My family told me, 'You have to think of the children now. You have to think of your-self. It's time now.' And accepting God's plan helped me do that, get better. I have to believe that whatever the reason, God doesn't let things happen that aren't supposed to happen."

The women said that all of the coping methods they used provided them some relief from stress, although their coping strategies were indirect rather than direct; that is, their coping strategies were attempts to influence their perceptions of the stressors rather than attempts to eliminate or change the actual sources of their stress. Because perceptions of both stress and relief from stress are highly subjective, the effectiveness of their coping methods could only be estimated from their descriptions of the distress they experienced despite using their coping strategies. In their discussions, it became clear that work, rationalization, denial, and reliance on religious faith provided only temporary relief.

Nearly all of the women said that, over the years of their marriage, they had experienced some periods of nervousness, anxiety, depression, irritability, and unwanted thoughts about accidents in the mines or injuries to their husbands. A few had occasionally experienced crying spells, periods of deep sadness, sleep disturbances of various kinds, allergy attacks, stomach upsets, and other physical problems. Several women had sought medical help for physical problems they believed were probably related to the pressures they felt they must accept as a part of their lives. One had gone to a psychologist to find relief from her feelings of nervousness, anxiety, and sleeplessness, and two others believed they should have done so.

Their most frequently experienced problems were anxiety and depression. They described anxiety in terms that made clear that these feelings were pervasive, troublesome, and sometimes intrusive. As one said, their anxieties were "like a little cloud that's always in the back of your mind." In contrast, they described depression as occurring periodically and varying in duration, depth of feeling and length of time between episodes. Feelings of depression were feelings of being "blue," "sad," "like I'm nothing," "heavy, tired."

Most of the women had no difficulty identifying the times and situations when they would be likely to feel anxious although depression was less predictable. The most common

and predictable anxiety-provoking situation, shift changes, occurred so frequently that the resulting stresses on the women
were repeated every second or third week. Other stressful occasions such as times when husbands were required to perform
unusual or unfamiliar mining tasks or when circumstances
suggested that a strike or layoff might take place soon, occurred
less frequently and at greater intervals.

The less predictable depressions seemed to the women to
occur without association with particular situations. In addition, the older women believed they experienced fewer
depressions than younger women because they had become
more accustomed to the continuing stresses. Younger women,
on the other hand, believed they experienced more frequent depressions than the older women but were doubtful as to
whether or not women could grow out of these feelings. Nearly
everyone believed that, on many occasions, their feelings of depression were deepened by the fatigue of caring for home,
husband, and children, and of working outside the home.

Lynn described her feelings of anxiety as "like being scared a
little all the time. . . . I am, I think, a little scared. It's in the
back of my mind that I don't know what might happen, and I
don't think I could take it. . . . I think about how much better
off I am than some, but that doesn't always help. I'm pretty
high-strung, I guess, but I can't even talk about it when I feel
that way. Last week he went on third shift, and he had to take
over for some other guy, and I started worrying before he even
went. He went to work tired, and those times I really worry. I
kept busy, but then near the end of his shift, I started watching
for him to come in. If I would've gone to bed, I would've waked
up at every little sound.

"If I think he's going out on strike, I think, 'How are we
going to pay our bills? . . . what happens if the baby gets sick?'
It's not knowing that makes it so bad. It always works out all
right, but then I just feel blue. . . . It's like being a little tired. I
don't want to do anything, don't want to talk to anybody. . . .
Sometimes I just sit. Before the baby came, a couple of times I
came home from work and just went to bed and stayed there
until he got home."

Some of the women who relied on keeping busy to help cope with anxiety believed that they were able to reduce their negative moods more quickly if they completely involved themselves in their work. Others, however, thought that work only occupied the surface of their minds rather than reduced worry, and that, underneath, the worry continued undiminished. Nancy said, "I get busy with my crafts, and I really have to concentrate, and if the phone rings I jump a mile. It helps to do this [craft work]. It helps a lot. I wouldn't give it up . . . it's something for me. . . . But I don't tell myself it keeps me from worrying underneath. What it does help is when I feel down, really bad . . . I come out here and work like crazy. . . . Then I feel better."

In contrast, Cora believed that in her case, "It's only as long as I'm busy that I'm not thinking about him and I'm not worrying. You got to give your attention *all the way* to something else. That's the only way to keep it out of your mind. And when you stop, it's back. . . . If you feel bad, depressed, it works the same. When something bothers you, you can give your attention to your children, your housework, to whatever you can really put your mind into, and that'll keep it out of your mind. But nothing takes it away all the way. . . . Everyone in their life has problems, but if your husband works in the mine, you got more. And nothing's ever going to take them away 'til he's out."

Although not necessarily associated with either anxiety or depression, irritability and nervousness were also frequently occurring problems for most of the women. About half of the women said such feelings were so frequent that they occasionally created serious problems in marriage or family interactions. Ginny was one of the few who sought medical or psychological help to alleviate her frequent nervousness and irritability. She described it as "absolutely necessary or I would have just gone to pieces. . . . I think I really did for a little. I would be so nervous I'd shake. I'd just start to shake and I couldn't stop. And I'd be so cranky other times I'd drive him and the kids crazy. Then I started having crying spells. I just wouldn't be able to stop. . . . One day I started to cry at my mon's house, and she said, 'You got to see a doctor and you got to do it now.' and that's when I got some help. I went to see our doctor, and he sent me to a therapist. . . . I know there's some that think that's ridiculous, but it helped me . . . and it helped my husband too, because he was really worried about me, and I felt even worse because of that."

Carol sought medical help when she began to have asthma attacks and periods of time when her throat would swell so much that she had difficulty speaking. "I used to get the feeling I couldn't talk about things . . . about his work or how I felt. It was too hard for me to put it into words. I got so I didn't want to know about it, but it helps him to talk about it, so I'd sit down and listen. Well, it helped him, but I just could not talk about anything to do with his job. Then I got to where I couldn't do it [listen] anymore, but I'd overhear him talking to his friends or my son . . . things I don't want to hear about. I told him, but he felt that not talking about things didn't help. He said I should talk about how I felt, but I couldn't . . . not to anyone.

"I got allergy attacks one year . . . from out of nowhere really . . . to house dust and grasses. Then I started with this thick throat to where I could only whisper. Then there was this accident in his mine, and he had a cousin died there. . . . That's when I got an asthma attack, and he said I had to go to the doctor. The doctor said I had all these allergies, but the worry made them all worse. Well, I could have told him that . . . but he gave me things to help and it got better. . . . It is better but I still have allergies. Sometimes I get really worried, and I feel like I'm going to have an asthma attack, and I worry about that. I read where if you are worried about something, you should just put it out of your mind. . . . Well, I can't do that. It just stays inside. I know some other women say, 'If you just work and pray, it'll go away.' Well, maybe that works for them. It don't for me."

Methods of coping with stressful circumstances were but one of the many kinds of responses to their environment that the women, like people everywhere, learned as they grew to adulthood. Much of this learning took place, first, through interactions within their immediate family and, second, in interactions with other relatives, peers, and teachers. The specific behaviors they learned reflected the ways that other people in their social environments had learned to deal with events. Their childhood families had had to cope with birth, death, marriage, parenting, sudden unemployment, illnesses and injuries, and the stresses and strains of the miners' occupations. As adults, the women coped with these events by using strategies that their parents, relatives, and other adults had modeled in their earlier social environments.

However, not all the possible coping strategies that might be used in these various life situations were likely to have been either modeled or available in the social environments of the mining families. A complex set of social and economic circumstances has been shown to be significant in determining the availability of coping methods (Pearlin and Schooler 1978). Socioeconomic status, years of formal education, age, and gender all influence the availability of coping methods. For example, the more years of education a person has had, the more likely it is that she or he has been exposed to models of effective coping strategies. Male children are more likely than female children to have been taught to cope directly with circumstances. People of the middle socioeconomic class are more likely to view themselves as instrumental in shaping their world rather than as being shaped by it and consequently are more likely to use direct coping methods (Pearlin and Schooler 1978; Pearlin 1980).

The characteristics of the stressful circumstances experienced by the women's childhood families influenced the coping strategies they learned. Not all of the stressful situations imposed on their families levied the same pressures in the same way. Some situations, such as temporary layoffs, imposed conditions in which the immediate threats (e.g., loss of income, insufficient food) to the family were routinely addressed with direct and fairly routine coping strategies. To deal with these situations, a miner's wife could store resources in good times, reduce household expenses during periods of unemployment, and find outside employment to bring in an income when there was a temporary layoff. The underlying cause of the circumstances, the economic conditions or corporate attitudes that created the layoff, would not be addressed.

Other situations created higher levels of stress for their families, and direct coping strategies to address these circumstances were not known, not feasible, or not chosen because of their consequences. For example, direct coping strategies rarely addressed stress arising from the dangers of mining. Changing the nature of mining to eliminate the threats would not have been possible, and leaving the area would not have been desirable. Moreover, for most of the women's lives, the economy of their home areas offered few other means of earning an income sufficient to support a family.

In coping with occasional stressors such as the temporary layoff, most of the women relied on the coping strategies they had seen employed by their parents. Lynn said, "Well, I know my mother always had some money set aside for emergencies . . . like if my dad was off work for a couple days or someone got sick or something. . . . She'd have enough to take care of small emergencies. I don't think she ever even told me that. I just . . . knew it, I guess, so I just started doing that right away when we got married. I don't think I really planned it or anything. I just started doing it. It's not a lot, but it's enough that we don't worry about paying a doctor or replacing something small. . . . It's annoying when something happens, and I worry if it's the baby who's sick or if it's him [her husband], but it's no big deal. You just have to be prepared for small things like that."

Flo used the same method in times when money ran short. "It's a part of being a good wife, I think. My mother had a big family, and I think I copied her a lot. . . . She'd never throw anything good away. She'd say, 'You never know when you might need it,' and there were lots of times when we did. . . . Or she'd help some other family. We learned to set something aside, make do, and take care of the problems that came up . . . in lots of ways that really came in handy for me later on. I don't think anybody ever got upset at little things. My mother'd say, 'If you get upset at little problems, you'll be upset all the time,' so I learned to be prepared, to just be ready to take care of things and not get upset about them. It was just a part of life . . . and you learned to deal with it."

When stressful situations such as temporary layoffs were repeated frequently, the resulting family tensions revealed the temporary and incomplete nature of relief that came from coping with immediate threats rather than the underlying circumstances. Nevertheless, these situations were also often the situations in which direct coping would not have been perceived as either feasible or desirable. Beth remembered from childhood that "My mother always knew when my dad came home if he was laid off again. . . . Maybe she'd heard from a neighbor or she'd guess just from the look on his face. He'd feel bad but she'd . . . well, not really be mad but irritated, frustrated, I think. She'd talk about how they used the men, just like animals, never giving them nothing extra, charging them for everything they got, and not telling them until the very last minute if they wasn't going to go back the next day. Like I said, she wouldn't really be mad at *him*. It wasn't his fault, he couldn't do anything to change any of that. No one could.

"But we all knew what she thought about it and how she felt. It made me feel bad then. . . . I didn't understand it, but now I've felt the same way lots of times . . . and said the same things. It gets you that no matter what you do, you can't feel it won't happen again. Things are better now, but you really can't change it much. . . . You could maybe move somewhere, but no one wants to. He still gets laid off. There's still strikes. Companies don't think of anything but money . . . never about the men who make it for them. When he gets laid off, I feel the same way she did. And I do the same things she did to get by . . . pinch money, put up stuff [preserve food], make do with what we've got."

Mary remembered her family's reactions to frequent layoffs as "times when everyone had to pitch in and do more. . . . We always had a garden—we still do—and in the mining camp everyone helped everyone else. But we always heard about what was going on. When the men was off, nobody talked about anything else, and people would get pretty mad about it. . . . My dad would say the company kept us down, over and over. People got scared too if it went on long. My mother

would say we've got to be like little soldiers. We got to keep
going and do what we have to do to get by, and the Lord will
provide. I learned that from her . . . to keep on going and do
what you have to do . . . take care of yourself and your family,
'cause the company didn't care anything about the miners'
families. Now, well, now it is better, but you can't make the
work steady. . . . . You can't make it safe. . . . This is your life."

Highly stressful situations such as accidents in the mines
created dramatic and emotional situations in which the coping
strategies demonstrated by families, and attitudes about
the causes of the situations, became indelible memories. The
women raised in mining camps recalled, "Even when you're
little, when that siren goes, you know someone got hurt. It's
a feeling you never forget. Everyone come running to the pit
mouth, and it's a feeling that nobody could really express. . . .
You want to know who's hurt. . . . You got that feeling inside
that you don't want it to be yours. You never forget that.
Even now when that siren goes, you know, and that feeling
comes back."

Mary remembered that "my mother always said, 'Pray . . .
pray that God will take you through.' I saw her cry too, crying
and praying at the same time . . . and I've done that myself on
some days. I couldn't even count how many. You pray. What
else can you do? And after we knew they was all right, or yours
was . . . then you try to help them whose men did get hurt . . .
sometimes weren't coming out . . . and you prayed for them.
My mother would feel real bad sometimes after. Then she'd go
and sit on the front porch, and my dad would try to make her
feel better . . . tell her not to worry so. But . . . she knew all he did
and how hard it was underground, but there wasn't anything
else for him to do, and there wasn't anything she could do."

Some of the women learned direct coping strategies as
children that, as adults, they chose not to use because the consequences of eliminating or changing the source of stress had
become unacceptable. Sue explained, "I didn't really know
much about it, not being raised in a mining family. Oh, if
you're raised around here, you know, you read about it. You
hear about it but just from what other people say, not from

your own family, so . . . I wasn't prepared for any of this. My mother never had to cope with it, and when we had some big problem, she just found a way to get us out of it. . . . My dad too, when he had real problems at work, he found a way to get rid of them . . . and one time, he even got another job. When he died, my mother went out and got a job. We never had problems that went on day after day . . . that you couldn't fix."

"My mother used to tell me if things bothered me, fix them, and if I couldn't fix them, put them out of my head. . . . But, I'll tell you, it doesn't always work. I can't deal with things the way she did. . . . It's something you can't fix. Sometimes the only thing that helped was just not thinking about it, and that doesn't always work either. He hurt his back last year, and I couldn't keep that off my mind. . . . And he kept talking about it . . . how these rocks just came pouring down and he was getting out as fast as he could. . . . He was scared, and the rocks just kept coming down behind him.

"How can I put that out of my head? I even dreamed about it. No one can fix that . . . and if I want to be with him, I just have to deal with it, because he won't leave it. He's proud of what he does. I'll tell you, I had to learn about this first hand. Nothing ever prepared me to deal with the kind of job he's got. Maybe you get used to it if you're raised in a miner's family. . . . Maybe you learn how to accept it. I can't, and if I could have just one thing I wanted, it'd be for him to have another job."

All of the women believed their coping strategies had helped them to varying degrees to accept what they perceived as the unchangeable conditions of mining life. Nearly all had accepted the necessity of working within those conditions to make their lives and those of their families as peaceful and nurturing as possible. They were aware that their coping methods provided at best only temporary relief from the worry, tension, frustration, depression, and sometimes deprivation that seemed inseparable from the lives of mining families. Nevertheless, most continued to support their husbands' wishes to work in the mines.

There was general agreement that, if women married miners, they could look ahead to certain circumstances as inevitable.

Rose believed that anyone raised in a mining family or, indeed, in a mining area such as the area around her home "knows what you're going to have to do . . . what kind of life it is. You know it's going to be hard. If you don't know it, you learn it . . . learn you can't carry all of it in you all the time. You just have to take it one day at a time, get through each thing, do the best you can, take care of your home so you can feel good about that, take care of your children and see they grow up right, and trust in the Lord to see you through.

"If you know mining, you know it's going to be that way every day until he gets out of the mine to stay. You'll never know what is happening down there. You'll never be able to make it any different. You can't make him any safer. You can't hold the mountain up. You just do what you can do at home. You take care of yourself . . . and him. You try not to worry. You do what you have to do to ease your mind and his, so you can feel good about yourself. . . . And that's all anybody can do."

Despite the general consensus, there were some differences in opinions and attitudes between the older and the young women. Nearly all of the older women accepted the notion of the miner's wife as a nurturing, supportive subsidiary to her husband's choice of occupation. Their coping strategies required a great deal of conscious effort, and, looking back, they felt pride in the energy and determination they had shown in being good wives, mothers, and partners in such difficult circumstances. Nevertheless, not all of the older women believed these traditional role behaviors would, or should, continue to be characteristic of marriages in mining families. A few, such as Cora, expressed support for the refusal of their daughters or daughters-in-law to accept the same burdens as their mothers and grandmothers.

Younger women, that is, women younger than their mid-forties, expressed more discontent with the traditional notions about a miner's wife's role. They believed their exposure to changing social attitudes about women's roles in marriage and parenting and women's rights in general caused them to question the old notions and resent, if not resist, some aspects of their lives. They had, as Ginny said, "a different way of looking at this. . . . His mother didn't know anything else, but I know other people don't have it like this. I have a friend who's going to go to school, and her husband is just going to have to help take care of things even if he don't like it. Women have to have some choices. You can't spend all your life doing for somebody else."

The younger women expressed more annoyance and frustration over the necessity of having to routinely and repeatedly employ deliberate coping strategies to get though their day-to-day lives. Their words reflected anger and frustration because of the unfairness they perceived in their marriage relationships and their inability to change their life conditions. Their anger was sometimes directed at themselves or their husbands, sometimes at the coal companies, and sometimes at the seemingly uncaring attitude of the state. Their emotional responses also reflected the futility of years of coping with the same situations over and over. For a few there was also some resentment over unfulfilled personal expectations.

Karen believed her feelings were common among younger wives. "This wasn't what I thought being a wife would be like. . . . I guess my ideals were all off, but being a miner's wife isn't a fifty-fifty thing. . . . It's more like I'm the one who's responsible for most things, and it just makes me irritated. It all comes down to his job. . . . That's what sets our life up like it is, and he won't change. . . . And there's nothing here or even around he could change to, so it's the mine that makes our problems . . . and no one, no one, cares enough to try and make it different. The companies don't care. The state don't care . . . and I'm the one who has to cope with it every day. I can't really tell him how I feel, because I don't want him thinking about anything down there except his job. I'm the one who worries. I'm the one who has to be mother and father a lot. But this isn't the way I wanted my life to be. . . . It makes me so angry to think abut it, so I don't. . . . I can't. . . . If I thought about it every day, thought about how it's never going to change, I'd be mad at everybody every day. But it's still there . . . underneath.

The coping strategies the women used, the temporary nature of their effectiveness, and their knowledge that other women used similar strategies with similar results were all integral parts of the emotional complexity of their daily lives. Surrounding their daily lives was the context of their heritage with its focus on surviving in difficult circumstances. The coping methods they learned were aimed at fulfilling the principles of this heritage. They learned how to endure in adverse conditions and to feel pride in accomplishing that feat. They learned (even though the younger women expressed resistance) that a husband's occupational desires would take precedence over family considerations. They learned to accept the idea that many of the conditions of their lives were unchangeable, and made few or no attempts to escape this perception.

The acknowledgment that many of their life conditions were unchangeable was not the result of a passive nature. In most of the routine and nonroutine circumstances of their lives, the women were active, assertive, and instrumental. Some had taken part in demonstrations, picketing, and other active means of resisting the coal companies' decisions. Yet their recognition of their inability to make changes in many of the major sources of stress in their lives was realistic. The physical requirements of the mining process and the economic and political framework of the industry had changed in the past only in response to considerations of profit. Probably only considerations of profit would cause a change in the future. Having grown to adulthood in a tradition where home, family, and home area were too highly valued to leave, the wives felt that their course had been largely set. They had to learn to cope with the unchangeable because, as many women said over and over again, "What else was there to do?"

Moreover, the women's perceptions of their place in the overall society were also realistic. They, their parents, their children, and grandchildren were all part of a society in which those who produced materials to meet the basic needs of the society were devalued because of the nature of their service and often put at a disadvantage by those who received both the service and the profits. Their assessments of the nature of the relationships between themselves and the larger society, and of the role of the coal companies in these relationships were insightful and critical.

SIX

Today and Tomorrow: Company Issues and Personal Issues

When conversations with the miners' wives turned to the subject of the coal companies, the women described a relationship between themselves and the companies that was complex and deeply emotional. Built from years of mistrust, oppression, and sometimes violent conflicts (Brooks 1973; Corbin 1981; Maggard 1990a; Naughton 1988; Scott 1988), the tensions of this relationship lay beneath the surface of everyday interactions between the women, their husbands, and their families. The emotional nature of this relationship colored their perceptions of daily as well as future events. Discussions of the companies' effects on daily life suggested that, when the mines were working and the miners had no grievances, the tensions in the relationship were expressed primarily in complaints about work that was exhausting, dangerous, and carried out in adverse conditions. However, when miners were out of work, or an accident had occurred, or the company had acted to the detriment of the miners in one way or another, the deeper angers and resentments toward the companies surfaced and were openly expressed.

To an extent, the tensions in the relationship between workers, wives, and the companies were normative in the sense that dangerous and exhausting working conditions can also be found in other occupations that are highly stressful (Mellor 1986; Portner 1983). However, among the miners' wives, perceptions that the coal companies cared little for the miners and less for their families greatly increased the tensions arising from occupational characteristics. Many of the women made

comments to the effect that, at the local level, the coal operators "don't care" and, at the higher management level, "they
don't even know we're here, that it's us that makes the money
for them."

Mary illustrated her conception of the companies' attitudes
toward the miners by telling the story of her move from the
mining camp in which she grew up to the town in which she
presently lived. She said, "Hardly anyone lives in camps now,
but we all lived there when I was little. It was costing the
company too much to put up them little houses and keep up
with sewage and things like that. They didn't do anything like
that when I was little. . . . We got water from a spring at the
pit mouth, and you had an outhouse in back, but then it got
to costing too much just to do the little they did do. But you
had to pay rent for your house. You didn't own it. . . . They
wouldn't sell it to you until it started costing them money.
Then they came and told you you could buy your house if you
wanted.

"We had improved our house so much with our own
money, and other people did too. It was your home. Well, the
mine representative said, 'You have sanded floors, tile floors in
the kitchen, a cement walk, a basement, a shower, and an
inside bathroom.' Then they made our houses expensive to
buy. . . . more than you had to spend for one not in the camp!
But *we* did those things. I said to him, 'Who made the cement
walk? *We* did. Who made the picket fence? *We* did. Who dug
this basement out? *We* did. And now you want us to pay for
that? We'll move out first'. . . and that was that. So all of the
people began moving out. There wasn't that many homes to be
had then but we all went. Some came here. Some went into
the country. I don't know where everybody went but nobody
stayed. Nobody would stay because that's the way the company was. . . . Anything they could get out of you, they
would."

Other sources of anger and frustration quickly rose to the
surface when the women talked about the companies' attitudes
toward the miners and the strategies the companies had used
over time in managing production problems ranging from un-

derproduction to investigating accidents. Lynn said, "You know, it's this attitude that makes me angry. . . . It's just lots of little things that get to me. . . . Do they think we don't see it? Like green stamps . . . they give you green stamps when accidents are down, and they don't give them when accidents are up. They sent home a piece of paper to tell us about it. . . . It would say, 'So and so mine has had ten accidents and this one had one,' so some people get green stamps and some don't. This is supposed to get us to remind our husbands to work safely. It makes me so mad. . . . They wouldn't think of telling them not to rush, not to push, not to work on a different shift every couple weeks, but they'll push him to work harder and give me green stamps if he doesn't come home with his fingers smashed."

Her words were echoed by other women who spoke of the unreasonableness of continued shift work, of having miners work on unfamiliar tasks, of expecting them to work beyond their physical capacities, and of the uneasy and often failed balance between safety procedures and production pressures. Nearly every woman expressed similar feelings about these issues, and there was consensus that the coal companies, from the top ranks to the lowest "company man," had little or no concern for the workers. They believed this lack of concern had changed somewhat since the 1930s and 1940s but only because the miners' union had applied pressure, not because coal companies had become more caring about workers.

Adding to the conflicts that many of the women felt were their reactions to their husbands' foremen or supervisors who were former miner-colleagues. The transition from miner to company man was seen by most of the wives as bringing about not only a change in a miner's responsibilities but also a change in everyday attitudes and loyalties. The women believed that a company man would always remember the experiences and feelings of being a roof bolter or electrician but that his loyalties would no longer lie with his miner cohorts. In the mine he would have to carry out company edicts, implement and enforce company working strategies, and adopt company attitudes.

The miners' wives said that the miners who became foremen would direct their work crews to take shortcuts that they
themselves would not have taken before they became company
men. They also believed that, in order to demonstrate their effectiveness to the company, the former miners tried to push
their men beyond the efforts they themselves might previously
have been willing to make. A worrisome feeling for some
women was the notion that the company man would become
more rather than less tolerant of safety infractions in order to
maintain production rates. The women also made it clear that
their issues with the companies became particularly troublesome when the companies' lack of caring was expressed
through workers who had formerly been in the same position
as their husbands.

Laura and Paula believed that some of the irritation they felt
toward their husbands' supervisors and foremen arose from
safety and work production pressures and some from social relationships outside the mines. Laura believed that the company
men were "not as careful as they could be. It bothers me that
they used to be right there doing the same thing, but just because they're working for the company they don't see it the
same. I know he's come home and talked about how they
worked in places their supervisor never would have worked in
when he was working with them. They change when they go
with the company . . . and it's the same here, too [in the neigh-
borhood]. They may keep their old friends for a while but they
make new ones, company, after a while. . . . And some [miners]
don't want to keep friends with a company man either. It's a
big change, and some get, you know, a little upset about it
when someone you've known for ten years stops coming
around."

Paula agreed with Laura but saw the issue from a different
perspective. "It's a big problem with me because he wants to be
a supervisor some day. He's done most of the studying, and it's
what he wants. I don't want it even if the money is better.
When a man is a company man, he goes from one kind of thing
to another. . . . He's the company in there, not the man they're
[other miners] used to working with, and he's got to be re-

sponsible for everything that happens to them in there even if it wasn't his fault. If he gets to be supervisor, his boss sits in an office, and all the pressure is on my husband to keep up the pace and keep everybody safe. I know it'll mean we'll change friends, and that's . . . well, I could use more friends. . . . But it's not the same as having miners for friends. . . . It's different when they work for the company. I don't look forward to it, and I don't want him to be the one who's responsible for what happens when someone makes a mistake."

Over the years the strains between production pressures and safety measures (Althouse 1974) were foremost among the issues that created anger and frustration in mining families. Stories of the situations that resulted from production pressures were frequent in everyday conversations, and no one in the miners' families could avoid hearing about them. In nearly all of the women's families, it was as Rose said, "a big part of every day . . . and when something happens or almost does, you hear about it. You hear who got hurt and who almost did and what's not working right. . . . You hear the whole thing. You know when they're not mining enough coal and what places they went into that they didn't think were safe and all that. You might not want to hear it . . . how they were in such a hurry that so and so got hurt or this broke, and you might have things of you own you want to talk about, but you hear about his day."

While none of the women placed all the blame for these situations on the companies, and most considered carelessness the major element in accidents, they also believed that the pressures on the men to keep up high rates of production were instrumental in the miners' carelessness. Careless behavior included not only inattentiveness or unwillingness to use safety equipment but also failure to quit even when exhausted and failure to reject unsafe procedures or requests to work on relatively unfamiliar tasks. The women believed that the pressures on the miners came from the combination of stressful factors the men experienced. The strain of rotating shifts in combination with the exhausting physical labor of mining and the pressures of keeping up high rates of production was the cause of carelessness or inattentiveness.

Helen talked about these issues and the changes in the safety equipment and regulations that took place in the thirty years between the time her husband had begun in the mines and the time her son-in-law began. "There's been a lot of things that have changed, and I think things are much better now than they used to be. They teach them better for one thing, and then they have those masks to wear, and they do better ventilation, and they get taught how to keep themselves as safe as possible. But you know, a lot don't take the care they should. It's hard work and it's hot and dirty, and the masks make it hotter . . . and just more uncomfortable. And they take chances where they shouldn't or don't pay attention where they should. . . . I know because he's always told me about how they take chances when they shouldn't, or they're too tired to be careful, or they're just going to take one shortcut in fixing something. But the company blames them, and it's the company pushes them so they are tired all the time."

The coal companies' methods of investigating accidents and their power over state-level investigatory and regulatory practices were also elements in the tensions between the miners' wives and the coal companies. The women believed that accidents received only a cursory investigation at the local level unless there had been a fatality, and once an investigation moved above the local level, it became more of a political matter than an investigation into an accident. In their opinion, once politicized, investigations were easily shrugged off by the state, the mine, and even union officials. When fatalities occurred, investigations were less routine, but even fatal accidents became political events at the level of the state or the law court.

Amy, who described herself as usually quiet and uncomplaining, said that when her husband was killed in a mining accident, her miner father-in-law and her husband's coworkers were skeptical about the company's reassurances that the accident would be fully investigated. She also didn't understand why some of his coworkers avoided her. The company said there would be a hearing, the cause of the accident would be determined, and the blame would be laid where it belonged; and she believed them. She was told that the collapsed section of the tunnel where her husband's body lay would be opened, and that maybe they could find his personal items for her to keep. She felt that having something of his would make it easier for her.

"I guess I should have know from the way his supervisor wouldn't look me in the eye. . . . I should have known it wasn't going to be like the company said. First, they didn't do anything about it for a long time. Then they did have a hearing and it was a joke. It was a farce, just . . . a motion to go through. The state department of mines conducted the first hearing, and it was a complete farce. The man who was conducting it asked questions like 'What's your name? Where were you working on the day of the fire? But when he asked real pertinent questions, the company's lawyers would always object, and it just went on and on like that, and nothing came out. It was just for show. . . . And I knew what happened, because the other men finally told me, but they weren't allowed to tell it then . . . and they never were, never.

"I tell you, I made a complete pest of myself. I did things I never ever thought I'd do. I called people,. I wrote letters. People must have thought I was a complete idiot, but I pushed and pushed, and they had a second hearing. It came out how it happened at that hearing—the way the machinery was all covered with dust, the crack in the ceiling, they way the wires were pinched down to bare metal, and they were told to just keep on doing what they were doing. But, you know, the expression 'You can't fight city hall' is right. . . . The city hall is the coal company, and the second hearing's all that ever happened. . . . It all just was dropped.

"They kept telling me they'd try to open that part up like I said, but they never did. They never were going to do that. They just told me that, I guess. They never opened up that section of the mine, and my dad said they mined right up to it and around it, but they wouldn't open it up . . . the point where all the evidence is staying shut down. Then the two-year statute was up. You can't do anything anymore after that, so nothing can come of it. They won, I lost . . . and everyone tried to tell me it would be that way, but I couldn't believe it then."

Amy's story, in much the same way as Mary's story, illustrated the assessments of the coal companies that nearly all of
the women made. Coal was big and powerful. It controlled
state and local governments, was directed at the top by business entities oriented solely toward profit, and at the local level
by people whose livelihood depended on putting into practice
the company policies that maintained production. Amy and
the other women believed that whatever occurred at local
levels had no impact on any real person at higher levels. At the
top corporate levels the coal companies were, as Lynn described
it, ignorant of the workers who produced the profits. "You
think they care or know what goes on down here? I don't. They
live in a whole different world up there. They don't know anything but the profits. The people at the top sitting in their big
offices in the city, don't know there's people down here. . . .
We're tons per year, that's all. You think we can change that?
I don't."

The strikes that periodically disrupted work and income
were another major element in the tensions that existed between the coal companies and the miners' wives. Although the
wives tended to perceive company practices as the primary
cause of strikes, they also placed a part of the blame on the
miners and the unions. However, their recognition of the
miners' share of responsibility for strikes was tempered by
their understanding that solidarity on the part of the miners
was one of the few influential pressures that could be brought
to bear on the coal companies. Over the decades since the late
1800s, miners' efforts to change working conditions, improve
wages and wage structures, and increase the kinds of safety
measures that could be taken had failed repeatedly until the
miners began to organize and work together in the 1920s and
1930s (Knipe and Lewis 1971). The miners' wives sometimes
disagreed with their husbands over the issues that brought the
men out on strike, but they supported the miners' collective
actions, often with active individual efforts (Maggard 1990a;
Scott 1988).

The circumstances that contributed to the stress caused by
strikes were complex. The women said they were often critical

of the reasons given for a strike, but, at the same time, wished to support their husbands. The loss of the miner's income posed the threat of living on savings or on the much smaller income earned by the miner's wife. In addition, because the women did much of the work of budgeting and spending, the stress of having to devise a way to continue to meet financial needs was an additional burden on them. The final burden came from the necessity of working outside the home and also being responsible for the majority of the household and child-rearing tasks.

Cora laughed and said, "There's not many times I nag, but he knows I'm going to have something to say about going out, [on strike] for some little reason. . . . I think they have to sometimes, but it's the money that makes it hard. . . . And when the children were little and they'd go out, I had to work and still do everything here. Having a husband on strike does not mean you got another pair of hands at home, so I guess you'd say I had mixed feelings. I'd get mad about it, and he'd get mad at me, say I didn't understand. But I've gone out and picketed, walked in demonstrations, pestered them in the office, made up posters. . . . I've supported them. What the men don't understand is all the extra things it puts on the women when they go out on strike."

The miners were also under considerable strain when the mines went out on strike. They did not all always agree with the reasons for calling a strike, and stress arose from the strain of being out of work and at odds with company men and sometimes coworkers, with whom they might have worked for years. They were often unsure of what the next days or weeks would bring, and they were also a part of an emotionally charged group situation. These circumstances created tensions among the miners, and the women believed they heightened tensions at home.

Louise said, "I can't stand it if he's home for longer than a day or two. He's irritable, he's in and out, doesn't know what to do. He's angry. Usually he doesn't want to be out, but he's got to support the ones who go out. And we just both begin to get on each other's nerves to the point where sometimes I just go out . . . visit my friend or something. . . . It gets worse as the money goes too. There's money you can get if it goes on [strike benefits], but it takes forever to get it, and you have to buy food and pay your bills. You can't just wait for that . . . and it isn't much. I worry about using up our savings and I get irritable too. It gets so bad sometimes I'm glad when he goes out [of the house]."

When strikes grew lengthy and money that had taken months to save dwindled, the family faced the dilemma of no money coming in, a nearly empty savings account, and continuing living expenses. These problems not only created anxiety but also, over time, caused husbands and wives to feel hopeless about their ability to support a family. Although, over the years of their marriages, they achieved financial stability again when strikes ended, each new strike renewed the cycle of tension and anxiety. Many of the women found it difficult to maintain an optimistic view of their family's financial future.

The tensions that arose during these times were also expressed in occasional aggressive interactions between workers and coal companies. The deep angers and resentments that miners and their families harbored for years rose easily to the surface to generate verbal and physical confrontations that never appeared to end with any lasting peaceful resolution. The tensions the women and their families experienced during strikes were alleviated slightly because they worked together to confront the companies with their collective pressures. Nevertheless, all of the women had known families who lived in poverty because there was no work. There was no protection from the frequent anxiety arising from the fear of long-term unemployment.

Young and old alike, the women believed their attitudes and feelings about themselves and their world had undergone considerable change over the years. The older women had lived through times of significant change in the major social systems of their communities, state, and nation, and they were aware that these social changes had altered their outlooks on life. They described their inner growth over these years as "getting smarter" and "seeing more," a change that included not only greater tolerance of people and social trends but also more skepticism toward both. They felt they had become more aware of the complexities and contradictions of society and politics and had gained a greater awareness of themselves relative to others.

Paula reflected on the ways in which she believed she had changed and explained, "A part is just growing up and a part is learning about how things are. . . . You know, you learn just from being around people, from reading, and lot from just listening to what people say. You have to deal with things in your life, and you learn from that. You learn everyone isn't what you think, and it might even be someone close to you. You might find out everyone doesn't think like you think they do. Nothing is as easy as you think it is when you're just fifteen or sixteen, and nothing is as, well, simple. And when you have children, you have to make yourself start to think differently . . . because of them. That teaches you a lot. I'm a lot different now. I'm older. I'm smarter. I don't trust everyone anymore, but I think it's easier to get along with other people."

The women, particularly the older women, knew they had been instrumental in shaping the events of their lives. Yet, they did not feel that they could have made substantial changes in their life conditions. Acceptance, not despair, underlay their conceptions of the way their decisions shaped their lives. Mary and Beth both believed, "You grow up with everything in your life leading you in one way. . . . You live the way you live because you grew up in a mining camp. You marry the man you marry because that's who you know, raise your children the way you think best because that's what you know. Maybe there's other ways to be but you don't know them.

"You might read in the paper that other men have better jobs, other people work for companies that take care of them better. But your life is here. You can work to make things better. . . . I went all the way down to Charleston to get better things for my children in school . . . to get them paper and pencils. . . . You can make some changes—I got other women together and stood up to the school board. But you can't change the economy because you don't know how. And you can't change the coal operators because you don't have the power and the money, and you're just one person or fifty, and you'd have to change the whole country to make it better."

Mistrust of the broader social system was expressed primarily by younger women. They described growing doubts and skepticism about their social systems that had begun early in their adulthood and had deepened to include a general mistrust of social and political authority in its many roles. These doubts influenced their understanding of ongoing political and social events. For many, there was an underlying feeling of having been misled by what they had been taught about society. They were angrier than the older women.

Ginny expressed her feelings about the local political atmosphere as "sort of generally not in favor of what they want to do most of the time. They look the other way when all the college students are breaking the laws, but let someone like us do it and they wouldn't look the other way, you can bet. They all want you to believe they're going to make things better, but what they want is to get elected. That's not what your government is supposed to be—it's supposed to be taking care of you. . . . What they do here is cater to the coal operators— they're God—and to the college students. I have a hard time believing anything any of them say anymore."

Karen agreed with Ginny and added, "It's supposed to be the voters who decide, but you know it isn't. . . . And politicians are all the same. They want the money and the place and all the publicity, but once they get there, they don't know you. I used to think workers got what they deserved. If they wanted it better then they had to fight for it. . . . Now I see that you can fight and get nowhere . . . that there's people in factories and driving trucks and working in construction that can't do any more than the miners can. It's not supposed to be that way, and when I read what these politicians say, I just get mad."

All of the women were aware of having grown and developed in their roles of wives, mothers, and workers. They attributed much of this growth to having had to "deal with" all of the events of their daily lives as well as the larger and more stressful life events. They did not perceive growth as an automatic process that proceeded steadily over time but as change that made itself known from time to time. Sharon described it as analogous to a series of peaks and valleys. She said, "The hard times make you struggle to get over them. Sometimes it seems as if you never will, and . . . well, sometimes it seems like it just doesn't matter anyhow. But sometimes later when things like that come around again, you see it different. . . . You know you learned something even if it's just to keep on. . . . You know you can.

"Sometimes you even feel different. . . . He got hurt bad once, and after that I've never felt the same about his job. He wanted to change, go to another mine, and we were out of work for a month then. I was scared he wouldn't get in anywhere, and after he did, I think I saw his job and my job different. . . . I saw my job meant more. He wasn't there long and they went out on strike. . . . I knew what we'd do, and I felt better about it, more secure, I guess. When you have to deal with things like that, it changes you even if you don't know it at the time. You know more. You see things you didn't see before. . . . Or maybe you saw them but it didn't mean something until after you went through something hard."

Most of the women, young and old, had seen the changes in themselves as positive, as having made them stronger, better able to cope with the world, and more knowledgeable about themselves. However, a few had experienced repeated situations in which they felt they had failed to cope as well as other women, and they attributed their failure to an inner inadequacy or a lack of experience at being a miner's wife. One woman believed that she not only lacked some inner strength that other miners' wives possessed but also that growing up in a nonmining family had left her unprepared to cope with the situations she encountered during her marriage.

There were, she felt, "too many times when I just can't deal with it and then let it go. I get so depressed when things go wrong . . . if there's a strike, or if he's being more tired than usual, or if he comes home with his back hurt, or if there's been an accident, [or if] someone else got hurt even a little. I really don't handle it well. I just can't accept all this, and I get so depressed. I'm really a nervous kind of person, I always have been . . . and I didn't grow up with all this. I didn't know anything about mining, didn't want to. . . . When things are bad, they're on strike, or there's been some kind of trouble at the mine, I see other women and they handle it. His mother says, 'Don't think about it. Don't let it get you down so much.' . . . Well, I can't. I sit at home and cry."

For some, particularly the older women, their efforts over time to cope with the stresses of being a miner's wife eventually transcended any earlier resentments or feelings of unfairness and created a feeling of acceptance of their place in society and the experiences that accompanied it. This acceptance was not expressed as a sense of helplessness, passivity, or unwillingness to confront oppressive employers. Rather, it was expressed as an awareness that life was complex, that no one would have her path clearly laid out for her, and that the best thing to do was to confront problems as directly as possible. When this was not possible, one must accept it and know that one's place and progress in life were ultimately determined by God's will.

Beth believed, for example, that her own actions primarily determined many events, although she also believed that God determined who lived or died and under what circumstances. "God has a plan for you, but you have to be responsible for yourself. Things go right or wrong by the way you act, the way you believe it's going to be. You can work at having control and make things better. Some things anyway, you can control. This [sense of control] is one of the things you change in. . . . I'm older now. I understand things better now. . . . Life in general is easier to see. I used to blame everything on other people, but I see it's me that put me here, keeps me here. I get to decide what I want to do . . . stay, go, work, spend the day doing something else. When he comes home tired and complaining, I tell him to quit, but he won't. It's his choice where to work. . . . It's my choice to stay here. . . . I worry about him all the time but everybody's got to make their own choices. . . It isn't any different for my children. . . . It won't be for my grandchildren."

The women of these mining families did not think that the economic and social context of their lives would change much in the future. They believed that concerted, persistent effort over time could possibly force some changes on the mining industry. But they also felt that such changes could occur only if there were changes in attitude among the miners, and they were not optimistic that this would happen. Further, they felt that they would be the only ones to pay much attention to the needs and place of mining families in the larger economic and social system. Nevertheless, they hoped for an easier, safer, less stressful life for their children and grandchildren.

Given the predictions that little would change in the larger economic and social world, they predicted little change in the structure and experiences of their everyday personal lives over the next decade. In the past, they had chosen to become homemakers, child rearers, incidental-income earners, and the creators and maintainers of strong home- and family-based support systems. Nurturing their husbands and children came first; their own needs took second place. In the future, unless they became unable to bear the strain, the hierarchy would not change until children were grown and husbands retired. The women's liberation movement caused some younger and older women to criticize their traditional lifestyles, but for the most part the wives thought that this movement had little to do with them.

The older women were much more aware than the younger of the extent of the large changes that had taken place in the mining industry since the early 1900s and of the relatively small changes in family structures and roles. In their opinion, "Coal operators won't make any change that don't get pushed on them. You never see them thinking ahead of what will be good for the miner. . . . It's what will make more money. It's the miners who've made the operators change, and it's just so much better than it used to be. . . . They used to go in there alone and work from before dawn to dark. They worked hard. They didn't have it then [in the 1930s] like they have it now. Then they had ponies that pulled the cars out. . . . They used their muscles and a shovel and blasted it out and loaded it up by themselves. Now [in the 1970s] they've got machinery and they've got showers and they've got the union to look out for them. There's not a lot more they can do except get rid of shift work and maybe get more safety equipment. It'll never be safe. It's always going to be dirty hard work, the worst you can get.

"Families have it better now too because the miner makes more money and there's strike benefits and black lung benefits. But that's the money, and at home, a wife's got to first see to her children and then her husband . . . keep them happy, do what you can to help them not worry about you when they're down there. A husband is the most part of your life, and if he's a miner, you have to do what you can to make him as safe as you can, because you don't know what's going to happen. Being a miner's wife is not like anything else. That'll never change."

One aspect of change in the social system that created widely varying opinions among the women was the acceptance of women as miners. Some women argued adamantly that mining was men's work and women had no place in the mines. They used all of the usual arguments against women as miners: women were not as strong, they would be treated differently by the men, and this would create more hazards. Others argued not in favor of women as miners but in favor of a woman's right to support her children. Beth said, for example, "If a woman has no other way to earn a living for her children, she should be able to work in the mines if she can do the work. If I had no way to put food on the table for my children and I think I can do it, I'd feel like they shouldn't be able to say 'no.'"

Only a few younger and few older women believed that women should be able to find work at whatever occupation they wanted and were able to do. Karen said, "I'd never go down there, and I hope he doesn't ever have to work with any women. . . . I'd worry that if there was an accident, they wouldn't be able to help him or maybe he'd get hurt helping them. But I don't think it's *right* to say that women can't work in the mines if they want to. I wouldn't want someone telling *me* I couldn't work there just because I was a woman. A woman's got to earn a living too, and if she wants to work down there, they should let her if she can do it."

Few of the women perceived working in the mines as a preferred occupation for anyone, and most did not want their sons or daughters to become miners. Those who wished their children to work in occupations other than mining looked to education as the most immediately available answer to the problem of finding an occupation outside the mines. However, they were skeptical of the school systems' ability to provide the most useful education for their children, and they tended to think that state and local governments did not use school funds wisely or demonstrate real concern for their children's future. There was, they felt, too much money spent on "things like sports and trips and clubs" and not enough on good vocational education.

In the past, some had confronted school officials at the local and state level and had demanded better use of money intended for education. Years ago Mary had asserted herself to get educational funds for her children. She had, she explained, "found out there *was* money for paper and pencils and things they weren't getting. . . . They made us pay for those things, and the ones whose families didn't have the money to buy them didn't have any . . . but the money was there. It just wasn't being used! I talked to everybody, I called, I wrote letters, I got other women to write letters, and I went down there and argued that the money wasn't being used right." Mary achieved her goal but only with a great deal of time and effort spent in organizing other women to join in her campaign of phone calls, letters, and visits to state education official. Mary other women, particularly those with very young children at home, never felt the determination or did not have the energy to force improvements in the system.

There was a general consensus that the school systems were much better now than they had been decades ago but that the influence of the mines on education was unchangeable. Getting children to school and keeping them there could depend on whether there were long strikes or shutdowns or, in good times, on the wages the mine paid. Long strikes and shutdowns meant little or no income for the family, and in those times nothing could be spared for clothes, shoes, and other school expenses. Middle-aged and older women remembered the struggle their parents had had to keep them outfitted for school and how difficult it was to accept the eventual decision not to continue because they could not buy shoes, dresses, and books. Economic times were not as severe as they had been when the older women were children, but it was not unusual even for contemporary mining families to be without the funds to purchase shoes and clothes for school when the mines were on strike or shutdown.

In one respect, the situation had improved for families with school-age children—the school systems provided more for children than they had when the older women were in school and the wages families earned were much higher. However, when economic times were good for the coal operators and the mines were working steadily, the attraction of good wages drew young people away from school and into the mines. There were few occupations for young people that paid wages higher than those that could be earned in the mines, and a miner did not need a high school diploma.

What the women wanted for their children and grandchildren did not differ from the wishes of parents and grandparents anywhere: an education, a job that paid a living wage and did not threaten to take their lives or health, a happy and mutually supportive marriage, healthy children, a home. They knew these goals were and would remain hard to reach. Each woman, from the youngest to the oldest, had had to work hard to move toward these goals, and they thought it unlikely that their children and grandchildren would reach them easily. They hoped the struggle would not be as difficult for their younger people as it had been for them, but their dependence on mining for their livelihood created an underlying pessimism.

Among the problems the women foresaw for themselves and their children was decreasing support from family and social networks. Despite the continuing closeness of family ties and the support of church, neighbors, and other miners' wives during times of strike, injury, or death, the support networks that formerly provided emotional sustenance had been weakened by social and economic change.

The tightly knit support networks provided by mining families living side by side in the mining camps had disappeared along with the mining camps. Wage increases over several decades had encouraged mining families to purchase better homes in the small towns and rural areas around the mines. Consequently, mining families had dispersed into more occupationally heterogeneous neighborhoods or into areas where few other families lived. Parents, siblings, and friends might be miles away, and miners' wives who did not work outside the home or did not actively seek out other women might see few other people except in stores or at church. Even in the local churches, the congregations included far fewer mining families than they once had, and the conditions the mining families must face were no longer understood by the preacher and the majority of the congregation.

Some of the younger women moved away from their former communities when they married or when they purchased a home. Over time they lost touch with friends. When children were young and husbands were working on changing shifts, visiting friends or family five or ten miles away, or having friends come in became more difficult. The telephone became their link to other women but, as Laura said, "It's not the same. . . . You can't run next door and have a cup of coffee and talk. . . . And somehow when you don't see each other, you don't talk about the things you used to talk about. I used to tell my friend everything, and she understood because her husband's a miner, but since we moved out here it's different. I'm here, she's fifteen miles away. . . . I really have no friends any more. . . . I'm just here with the kids. My mother had neighbors and friends close and so did his, I don't have anyone close."

Diminishing support networks not only left many women with few and distant friends, they also reduced the availability and usefulness of older women as models of ways of coping with the stresses and strains of being a miner's wife. Such models could be particularly important for women who did not grow up in mining families and who married with little or no knowledge of the conditions that mining created for families. Nancy, for example, believed that much of the stress of her first years as a miner's wife had been reduced through the relationships that developed between herself and her husband's mother and sister.

"I never knew about mining. I grew up on a farm and never lived around miners. I didn't know how they had to work and how dangerous it was, but his dad was a miner, and so was his granddad. His mother used to tell me how it was when she was a child and how she got through strikes by saving and working and making things at home. I could talk to her. She understood, and I never asked for help but it was always there when we needed it. She'd hear about something at the mine and just show up. . . . First time he got hurt, someone called her first and she just showed up here and said, 'Go to the hospital. I'll stay here and take care of things.' I know some don't have that kind of family close, but I don't know what I would have done without them."

Another consequence of weakened support networks was a reduction in the flow of information that passed from miners to their families and then from family to family. The older women, in particular, could recall when information about changing working conditions, management actions, and everyday situations moved quickly from home to home. As mining families dispersed into the towns and rural areas, information moved from miner to family but beyond each family only to the extent that the family interacted with other families.

Mary explained, "In the camps everyone knew what was going on all the time. . . . You knew who needed help, who got hurt, who was the best foreman. If someone had trouble with their child, you knew it, and if someone was sick, you knew it. If a man was treated bad by the company, you knew it. Now you hear it from your husband that someone got hurt, or that they're going to go ahead and mine where they shouldn't. . . . Or maybe you read about someone in the paper, and you feel bad about it, and you ought to help, but they live somewhere else. . . . You don't know them. . . . And a lot of times anymore people don't help each other out."

Amy agreed and pointed out that when her husband was killed in the mine and she asserted herself to have the investigation continued, her support came primarily from her husband's parents and from some of her husband's coworkers but not from other miners' wives or from neighbors. "The other women [whose husbands died] don't live around here. They cared but they're too far away to be really involved, and I was too far away from them to be involved with them either. My neighbors aren't miners. . . . They cared but they didn't know, didn't understand. My neighbors thought I was crazy, that the company was probably telling the truth. I felt I had to do it by myself and with the help of my in-laws. My father-in-law said it wouldn't have been that way when he was young and miners lived close together."

The lack of close similar friends could, and did, lead to feelings of loneliness and isolation for some women, but for others the lack of similar friends allowed for friendships among women who were less accepting of the mining way of life. Those who worked full time outside the home were particularly likely to have made such friendships and, consequently, to have been exposed to information contrary to the mining families' traditional view of women's roles.

Carol believed her ideas about women's roles had changed as a result of making friends at the commercial establishment where she once worked full time and, when we spoke, worked part time. "The other women there aren't married to miners so there's a lot they don't understand. . . . They don't know about how you can feel about him down there and why you feel you have to take the most responsibility around the home. . . . But they're good people and their ideas about things aren't wrong, just different. And, you know, sometimes they're right. One of the women who works there says, 'So what if your husband wants you to be home all the time. . . . You have a life to live too, and what you want is as important as what he wants.' Well, you know, I thought at first she was wrong. But then I thought more about it, and I changed my mind. . . . I think she's right."

While most of the women agreed that having acquaintances and friends among nonmining families had influenced their opinions, they believed that social and economic changes had caused many major modifications in their opinions and attitudes over the years and were likely to continue to cause more change in the future. Paula described these changes: "If you

look at how it is now, it's very different from the way it used to
be. People think differently about work and about what a wife's
supposed to do. It used to be that it took two people all the
time just to survive, but it's different now. A woman doesn't
have to sacrifice herself any more just to raise her children . . .
and a lot aren't willing to give up everything just to please a
husband. It's not about keeping to the way it's always been
done, it's about being treated like a human being."

Other women agreed. Sharon believed that, among the
younger couples she knew, "husbands sometimes don't like it
but we'll [the women] go right down to the company office and
picket in front of their office windows and stand out in front of
the mine holding a sign. . . . We're not afraid of them, and when
we get mad about things, we're going to do something to fight
back. We [she and Flo] started a little organization to get information out about what the company's doing. My husband at
first was kind of against it, but I've got a mind of my own, and
I'm not his shadow. . . . If I want to say something, I'm going to
do it. And if I were a woman who wanted to work in the mine,
I'd do it. People don't think anymore that women can't be what
they want to be. . . . I tell my daughter she can be anything she
wants to be . . . a doctor or a lawyer or whatever."

Most of the women predicted that even greater change
would occur in the future than had occurred in their past. They
saw the economy as playing the largest role in making changes
in the mining industry, and they expressed mixed feelings
about the future of the industry itself. Coal would always be
mined, they felt, but they were not optimistic about the place
of the miner. They also thought the state government had
played a losing game in its efforts to support the coal companies' grip on the workers. They believed the development of
the state's other assets would be the key factors in the future of
their children and grandchildren, and they hoped, again without optimism, that somehow the educational system would be
able to keep young people in school until they graduated.
Whether or not the future would bring positive or negative
change, they all agreed that change would come, as Beth said,
"on the backs of the men and women who live here."

Many of the older and younger women were decades apart in age, yet their experiences included the same threats and anxieties and the same hopes and wishes for the future. They sometimes questioned whether or not they would have the strength to continue to endure the daily stresses and strains that were so much a part of the lives of miners' wives. But, in times of major trials, they reflected on the difficulties their parents and grandparents had faced and believed that, like them, they would "get through" such times. As they said, "What else are you going to do? You can't just lay down and give up."

Although none of the women was highly educated, they were intelligent people who had no difficulty in seeing beneath the surface of the politics of mining to the personal motives of politicians. They believed the reluctance of politicians to take risks to help improve life for mining families testified to the persuasive influence of coal money and power. Their recognition of the limits of their ability to change conditions was based on fairly accurate assessments of the power of the miners vis-a-vis the power of the industry. On the other hand, as they looked back over the history of mining and compared past situations to current conditions, they also had felt that they and their children might be the last of the traditional mining families.

For now, however, they were, as Rose said, "proud of what we do. . . . And me, well, I'm proud to be a miner's wife. . . . Being a miner's wife is something to be proud of. . . . It ain't like being the wife of somebody in an office or a car salesman. . . . It's special . . . and we're special."

APPENDIX A

Personal Portraits

The women who shared their stories with us so many years ago brought different personalities and attitudes to the tasks of their lives despite their many shared ideas and perceptions. Rather than try to portray each woman, her situation, and her personality, I have tried in the following pages to describe women who were typical of the younger women, the middle aged women, and the older women. The young women, ranging in age from their early twenties to their late thirties, are represented here by Karen, Ginny, Nancy, and Paula; the middle aged women are represented by Flo, Amy, and Cora; and the older women by Mary, Rose, Beth, and Helen.

In general, the younger women had not anticipated how difficult, how tiring, and how all-involving the multiple occupations of wife/mother/homemaker would be. Each in her own way made accommodations to the demands of her married life.

Ginny, the youngest of the women, was still in her early twenties when we talked. She had had a great deal of difficulty in adapting to the workload and stress of homemaking and childrearing but thought it probably would get easier as she got older. Like most of the women, regardless of age, she was nicely but casually dressed and groomed. She was friendly from the first moment, cheerful and talkative. Her small white frame house sat close to the sidewalk on a residential street with many well kept small houses side by side. There was a tiny front stoop and, inside the house, a sunny living room furnished with homey and comfortable slipcovered chairs and a sofa. Plants basked in the light from a front picture window and a few magazines lay about on end tables.

Ginny's ideas tumbled out freely, accompanied by smiles, shrugs, and lively gestures. At times her cheerfulness changed to a rather tired stillness, and she cried when she talked about her fears for her husband's well-being. Her child and a neighbor's child played noisily in an adjacent room and occasionally would run into the living room to show her something they had colored or built. When they became too intrusive, she firmly shooed them away. She made it clear that her home, child, husband, and family were her world and admitted that she might need to "learn to be broader" as she got older. She said she found feminist ideas thought-provoking but didn't have time to deal with them for the time being. She also said rather sharply that the life situations of the women who write feminist articles must be worlds apart from her life situation and that if their lives were like hers they would not promote all the ideas they were promoting.

Karen was quieter than Ginny. She smiled often but she was less cheerful and seemed more introspective. Very big old trees shaded her trailer home on all sides. She said she'd like to cut a few down to let more light in but her husband wouldn't agree. Eventually, they wanted to build a home on the far side of their present lot, but work wasn't steady enough for the present to allow them to save the necessary money. She kept lamps lit in her living room, and the soft light showed books neatly arranged on a set of bookshelves, magazines stacked on the coffee table and end tables, and children's toys spilling out of their corners. Some of the magazines were women's magazines, some were mining and hunting magazines. She said she and her husband both read frequently. A Bible was prominent. She said she seldom reads it but she liked to have it there.

Karen felt an interest in feminist ideas and had concerns over whether she would be able to do what she wanted to do in the future. For right now, like Ginny, she deliberately and with forethought modified her wants to fit into her husband's occupational demands. Nevertheless, she clearly expressed her disapproval of some of the conditions of their life, and a listener had a sense that Karen was a little tougher and more demanding than Ginny, and a little more determined to satisfy her own needs.

Nancy, like Ginny, was talkative and cheerful. She was also quite assertive and more than a little skeptical that someone not associated with mining would have a sincere interest in mining families. Approaching middle age, she believed her experiences had shown her that working people have little support from anyone except other working people. She made no secret of her general mistrust of big business, politicians, and coal companies. She believed they had no conception of what life is like for miners and their families and no interest in anything but making a profit.

During our conversation, her husband brought coffee into the room and stayed to add an occasional comment. As Nancy talked, it became clear that she and her husband had had to struggle to save the money to buy this land, their spacious double-wide trailer with its plaid upholstered furniture, and their two vehicles. When they could afford to pay for more education for Nancy, she looked forward to becoming self-employed. Her voice was brisk and businesslike when she said her husband would have to accommodate to her needs then even if he was still in the mine. She did not look at her husband when she spoke and he made no comment.

Paula was also approaching middle age but said she would only admit to "late thirties." She laughed and said she would not have any birthdays after her thirty-ninth but would stay thirty-nine forever. Her small living room opened into a larger dining room, and both rooms had an almost formal look, with polished wood furniture and a carefully arranged abundance of knickknacks, books and magazines, still-life reproductions, and artful dried flower and wicker ornaments. From the front window of the square frame house, one could look down a long residential street to the busy community center below.

Paula's manner was very direct and matter of fact. She and her husband planned ahead for what they wanted and were "always busy." They had bought their house about five years before we talked and had worked together to make improvements ever since then. Paula had helped lay carpet, remodel porches, paint, and hang wallpaper. She said she could do an acceptable job of carpentering but her husband was both "handy" and creative, and she pointed with pride to an end table he had made the year before. She wanted to get the house "to where we want it" before the children were in high school. When that happened, Paula wanted to go back to college and finish her degree.

Flo, Amy, and Cora are fairly typical of the women who made up a loosely defined "middle age group," that is, women ranging in age from their early forties to their early fifties. Amy, in her mid-forties, was the youngest in this group, and Cora, in her early fifties, was the oldest. In general, the middle aged women had well formed opinions and often expressed strong interests in the business and politics of coal companies and local governments. They tended to react more intensely although with less mutual agreement than the younger women to issues such as equal employment opportunities and adequate wages for unskilled service jobs. They were also more assertive than younger women about the importance of their own needs relative to those of their husbands.

Amy was the quietest of this group but her manner was warm and friendly with none of the initial slight stiffness that preceded some interviews. Her white frame house shared a narrow and steeply sloping street with older houses in a variety of styles. Inside, she led the way into a bright tidy kitchen where she offered coffee and homemade cookies. She was immediately interested in what other women had had to say and, as she spoke of her own life, she occasionally poked fun at what she said were her own earlier ideas about marriage and homemaking.

Despite her quiet manner, she was not reluctant to share her feelings, ideas, and opinions. When she spoke of her close relationships with her family and her in-laws, the warmth of her feeling was clear. Her underlying strength became apparent when she spoke of her past conflicts with the mining company and her current efforts to find a way to get a better education and a better job. She would like a white collar job for herself and was determined to have one eventually. Her son's education had to come first, however, and she was adamant that he would not become a miner.

Flo's age put her in the middle of this "middle group" of women, but her energy, assertiveness, and quick blunt way of speaking made her stand out. Over time, her willingness to speak out on her opinions and to bring them to the attention of others had led her to think about going into local politics some time in the future when her children were all grown and settled. She brought the same bold energy to meeting the demands of being a homemaker and a miner's wife, and she took pride in the results. Flo's home was tucked back in shallow green hills that had once surrounded a small mine site. Brick facing and white shutters set it off from a close cut lawn. Inside, the house was attractively furnished with floral slipcovers and crisp white ruffled curtains at the picture windows. The living room and kitchen were spotless, and through the kitchen windows could be seen a garden as neat and tidy as the living room or kitchen. Only one thing looked obviously used, and that was the big Bible that lay on the table by an easy chair.

Flo was pleased that other people might be interested in learning about the lives of miners' wives but doubtful that much could be done to make their lives less stressful. She also doubted that the economy of the coal regions would improve given the pressures to produce energy in less polluting ways. Her predictions for the future of the area were much more negative than those of other women, and it was clear that this was an important concern for her. In the end, she said, the miners, the local businesses, and "from there on to the top" would have to rely on their faith to bring them through the bad times she thought lay ahead.

Cora's house was more isolated than most of the other homes. It lay nearly five miles back up a narrow country road just barely wide enough for two cars to pass each other. Her family had farmed as well as worked in the mines, and a large barn and several smaller sheds behind the rather worn-looking farmhouse were reminders of those times. Cora said she cared not at all for growing anything, not even flowers, but she did devote much of her free time to working on various crafts. She asserted quite strongly that she deserved "to have the time and take the time" to do the things she enjoyed. One of the old sheds had been renovated into a workshop for her crafts, and it was there that we talked. As our conversation moved along, Cora's hands were busy with a woven basket of her own design.

She expressed much interest in hearing about the stories of other women, particularly those who believed that their religious faith gave the most help in relieving stress. She told me of her own return to a once nearly abandoned faith in God and of some of the unusual extrasensory experiences that preceded it. On one occasion she had been forewarned, she said, of an accident that would happen to her husband. On another occasion, she awakened in the middle of the night, suddenly "knowing" that the car in which one of her children was riding had broken down on a lonely back road. She believed this sort of knowledge was God's doing. Eventually it led her to renew her faith and she began attending church regularly.

The older women's ages ranged from the middle fifties to "nearly eighty," although most were in their middle to late fifties. As a group, there was more diversity of general opinions and attitudes among the older women than among the middle aged or younger women. Nevertheless, the older women were more tolerant than younger women of some contemporary women's issues (women working in the mines, for example) and more emphatic that a wife's needs are as important as a husband's. They were also quite firm in their beliefs that a miner's wife had to do more for her husband than other wives must do and that, looking back, they would not have chosen any other life for themselves.

Rose was the youngest of the older women. In her fifties, she appeared to be a decade younger. Her manner was warm and firm, and when she talked about her life, it was often with wry humor. Her home had also once been a farm, and a fenced pasture and cornfields that are worked by a neighbor still surrounded the house. The house had had new siding added only a few years ago and still looked fresh and new. Rose helped with siding the house and said she was as good a home carpenter and plumber as most men but only a "so so" office worker. She enjoys doing volunteer work and for many years, when she could take the time, had done hundreds of hours of volunteer work at a local hospital "just talking and helping people."

Rose made it clear that the volunteer work was for her own benefit; it helped her to accept her life, to feel that she had some advantages, and that regardless of how little money or material things she had she could always do something for other people. She also strongly emphasized that women who have children to support deserve to have any job they can do and, where they do the same work as men, deserve the same pay. Her son-in-law had told her about how meanly women were treated by company men and miners when they first came to work in the mine where he worked, and Rose was irate. She told him he had better not act that way.

Beth was also in her middle fifties at the time we talked. Like Cora, her house was located far back in the country but, unlike Cora, her home was fairly new. A brick and dark wood ranch style house, it sat on top of a long round-sided hill and overlooked the humped and rolling hills on all sides. Inside, comfortable slipcovered furniture in styles from several decades ago and well worn carpeting contrasted with the newness of the exterior. Beth was talkative and optimistic. Now they had a much nicer house than before. One of these days, they would be able to get new furniture, except that now the mines were not "working too good at the moment." But they'd be working full time again soon. In the meantime, there were house payments, car payments, and insurance to keep up, and they were being very careful in order not to deplete their savings too much.

She said that she and her husband had had numerous disagreements because of his job but that there really was no way to make his job different and she certainly was not going to change her mind about the kind of work she thought it was. She had, as she said, "strong opinions." Nor would she consider changing her ideas about what a wife's responsibilities were despite the difficulties. She said if she could change anything about her life it would just be to make his job easier for him. That would make her job easier for her.

Mary was in her sixties when we talked. She and her husband lived in a modest older white frame house on a quiet residential street with many other older frame houses. The living room was small and a little crowded with upholstered furniture, end tables, lamps, and a large television set. The end tables and walls bore many pictures of her children and grandchildren and a few of her parents and her husband's parents. There was a college graduation picture of each of their three children.

Mary was well informed on local and state politics and was an articulate and analytical critic of the government, mining companies, and the nature of mining. She was outspoken about her support for the right of women to work wherever they could manage to find a job and do it well enough. At the same time, she said she knew there was no life like a miner's life, and women married to miners just had to adjust to it and accept it even if it meant they had to do more than their share of work within the marriage.

Mary's husband joined us as we talked. Now and then he added to Mary's comments or explanations, and sometimes he chuckled at her bluntly condemning statements about how the mine companies and the state government treated the miners. They both smiled when Mary said he was always happy as long as he had a good lunch and some Twinkies. For a while he talked about his childhood experiences in the mines, but it was obvious that he had difficulty breathing when he talked at length. He said he did not do much anymore except watch television and chat with the children when they came to visit. He said he probably had a year or so left now. He looked down at his gnarled, arthritic hands and said they'd done a lot of hard work but they were in better shape than his lungs. Mary watched him as he spoke but made no comment.

Helen was the oldest of the women; she said with a smile that she was "nearly eighty" and, up until a decade or so ago, had known all of the families in her area and their children and their children's children. Her husband had died of black lung, but by the time he died they had owned their small farmhouse and the few acres on which it stood. They had not had much else, "but we didn't owe anybody anything" and that made Helen feel more secure when he died. Despite arthritis and a limp from a badly set broken bone thirty years before, she maintained herself in her home, raised vegetables and flowers in her garden, and occasionally drove herself to church and to a country store a few miles away.

She said she loved being a homemaker. The chores of homemaking, the cleaning, cooking, and polishing were not only enjoyable but also had kept her from worrying about anything that threatened their lives. The only thing she thought she might have liked better would have been to be an elementary school teacher because she loved children. Some of the happiest days of her life were the days when she went to school with her children to help as a volunteer teacher's aide. Even after her children were in high school, she would volunteer in the elementary school just for the enjoyment of working with the children.

Helen was outspoken and spirited about the issue of women working in the mines. She agreed with many of the other miners' wives that, while she could not imagine why anyone would want to work there, if a woman had children to support and that was the only place to earn an adequate wage, then no one should keep her out if she could do the work. She pointed out that women have worked in the fields, in factories, scrubbing floors, lifting heavy things in hospitals, and why, if they are able, shouldn't they work in a mine? She said any kind of work is better than living on charity.

None of the women who talked to us about their lives as miners' wives would have fit into the stereotypes that are sometimes used to describe miners and their families. Their homes, the towns where they lived, their views on life in general, and their hopes for themselves and their children were much more the reflection of working peoples' lives in other areas than the fictional image of the poor, illiterate, shack-housed mining families. The grains of truth that stereotypes are built upon were present. They were undereducated and their economic stability was often threatened, with little promise of stability in the future. In the earlier decades of mining, from the late 1800s to the late 1950s, housing and general living conditions were so abysmal for many mining families that it took national pressures to force the coal companies to make improvements. And, in contemporary times, the coal industry had declined so severely that many mining families suffered long periods of unemployment and dependence on state funds for subsistence.

Nevertheless, in the northern coal areas of West Virginia in the late 1970s, the economic slump that was to come and the devastatingly long strikes that followed in many of the coal regions of the country had not yet occurred. The mines were working most of the time, employment in the mines could be found, and when work was steady or there were two incomes, a family could fare reasonably well. The images of the women and their lives as they are described here are accurate for those times. Like women everywhere, they were in many ways alike and in some ways unique. They were, as they said, proud to be the wives of coal miners.

APPENDIX B

Other Women, Other Occupations

West Virginia miner's wives are not the only women whose lives are marked by the stresses and pressures of rotating shifts or a spouse's dangerous occupation. Rotating-shift work imposes stressful problems on more than eleven million American workers and their families (Mellor 1986), while the wives and families of many other workers in dangerous occupations must cope with the fear that their loved ones will suffer injuries or death on the job.

Shift work is particularly common in activities such as mining or manufacturing where continuous production is the most efficient way to maintain profits. However, rotating-shift work is not limited to industrial workers or profit-making manufacturing. It is also frequently required of many types of service workers such as law enforcement officers, firefighters, and rescue workers who perform work that may be needed at any time (Mellor 1986; Schwartz and Schwartz 1975).

Although the effects of shift work on workers have received little attention, a small but growing body of information from researchers in industrial and organizational disciplines had consistently pointed to the harmful effects of rotating work shifts on workers and on workers' families (Elliott et al. 1986; Maynard and Maynard 1982; Simon 1990). The research supports the notion that the underlying source of stress for workers is the repeated demand to adjust to changing sleeping and waking schedules. When people must work on a schedule that moves around the clock in disregard of the body's natural rhythms, they must repeatedly attempt to sleep when their bodies have attuned themselves to waking activity and to be awake when they have been accustomed to sleeping.

Readjustments of natural body rhythms are demanded at two- to six-week intervals over many of the working years of the shift worker. Even workers who adapt with relative ease to the changing hours are likely eventually to become stressed by rotating shifts. Further, while day workers or night workers may anticipate weekends and vacations as time for catching up on lost sleep, for shift workers, weekends and vacations create additional disjunctions as they try to reestablish normal schedules.

For some shift workers, the demand to adapt quickly to changing work hours is made more imperative by the dangers of their work environment and the level of skill necessary to carry out their work. They may be required to maintain high levels of alertness and responsiveness, make quick, accurate judgments, or exert unusual physical effort to complete a task. In occupations such as high-steel construction, mining, commercial fishing, and many manufacturing tasks, workers are exposed to increased risk of injury and death if they suffer from fatigue or inattentiveness.

Similarly, in law enforcement, firefighting, rescue work, and hospital work, both the worker and the recipient of the worker's services are at risk if the worker is less alert and responsive. Nevertheless, sleep problems, along with difficulty in concentrating, inattentiveness due to sleep deficits, sleepiness during work, and persistent fatigue are common among industrial, manufacturing, and service workers. The consequences are serious—all these problems have been found to be related to increased accidents at work (Akerstedt 1988; Finn 1981; Simon 1990). It is an unfortunate, and sometimes tragic, paradox of modern labor conditions that in many of the occupations in which the workers' safety and the safety of others depend heavily on attentiveness, careful use of skills, good judgment, and quick responses, shift work is the modus operandi.

The stress imposed by shift work moves beyond the work place, however, and contributes to the development of problems at home as well. The workers' lack of time for family responsibilities and activities and the carryover of fatigue from work to home contribute to strains that affect other family members and the marriage relationship. Policemen and hospital workers, for example, encounter difficulties in maintaining normal marital and family relations because of their lack of time to address problems and engage in social activities. The situation can become even more intense when the shift worker's fatigue, irritability, or depression creates apathy toward family problems or the need to disengage from problems as a way of trying to reduce feelings of stress (Dunham 1979; Finn 1981; Hageman 1978; Schwartz and Schwartz 1975; Simon 1990).

As shifts rotate around the clock, the wives of shift workers, like miners' wives, must take on family chores by themselves or delay them until their husbands are free. Family activities of all kinds must be scheduled for times that fit the shift worker's hours or be carried out without the shift worker's participation. When the shift worker sleeps in the daytime, normal daytime chores may have to be postponed and modified so as not to disturb the sleeper. When illness or family problems occur during night shift hours, the worker's spouse must cope without the assistance of her partner.

The struggle to carry a double load of family responsibilities, to adapt to frequent changes of schedule, to accommodate to a spouse's needs to rest and relax, and still to maintain one's own emotional equilibrium can become the source of chronic stress (Maynard et al. 1980). Policemen's wives, for example, believed the demands on a spouse's time, his attitudes toward the family's needs, and his shift work were their major sources of stress (Elliott et al. 1985; Hageman 1978; Maynard and Maynard 1982).

Shift work increases the risk of injury or death to workers in many occupations; but in some of those occupations, such as mining, the nature of the work itself generates the underlying stress experienced by the workers' partners. Shift work intensifies it. Working environments that contain many risks to workers create anxiety and worry in the workers' families as well as in the workers. Enforcing the law, fighting fires, fishing in the deep, cold waters of bays and oceans, and even growing crops and food animals have always been carried out under conditions that can, and do, result in accidental injury or death.

The families of law enforcement workers, for example, have always had to cope with the threat of death or physical injury from assaults by law breakers. Today they worry about the risks of random, drive-by shootings, of being shot or stabbed by drug dealers, of being involved in automobile accidents as the result of police chases, and of becoming accidentally infected with disease. Similarly, firefighters have always been exposed to high risks of death or injury from burns, explosions, falls, or smoke inhalation. In the past few decades, they have become increasingly at risk of exposure to caustic chemical smoke from burning plastics or other synthetics and of injuries caused by objects thrown by the crowds that attend fires in the cities.

Some occupations such as fishing or farming that may appear to present relatively fewer hazards have always been, in actuality, occupations with high risks for health and safety. The wives of fishermen along the Chesapeake Bay and off the coastal waters of Newfoundland, for example, have always worried if their husbands did not return when expected. They knew that every year some men drowned. Boats could capsize in the sudden storms that blow across the waters with too little warning to reach safety. A man might fall off a boat or be pulled off accidentally, and, even if he could swim (and many could not), his clothing was so heavy he was at great risk of drowning. In the winters along the Chesapeake, boats might become icebound, crushed, or lost in the fog (Davis 1983, 1989; Peffer 1979; Whitehead 1979).

Like the miners' wives, other women whose husbands faced frequent dangers in their daily work had to learn to cope with the stresses of their husbands' occupations and to rely on themselves to establish daily routines to maintain their families and homes. Feelings of tension, irritability, periods of depression, difficulty in sleeping, and feelings of doubt about whether they could continue to cope with their lives were not uncommon. Some were bothered by periodic physical ailments, less serious discomforts, or longer term ailments attributed to nervous conditions (Davis, 1983; 1989; Scott, 1988).

Many of them believed that no one but a woman in a similar situation could understand the difficulties of their lives, and many found the support of similar women a source of comfort. They discovered that developing an interest in activities other than homemaking and sharing that interest with other women alleviated some of the combined stresses of worry and overwork. Some women found that working outside the home relieved a portion of the tension, and a few found that pursuing interests in learning new occupational skills for the future also helped relieve stress.

Overall, the methods of coping employed by the wives of other workers in hazardous occupations differed little from those of the miners' wives. The wives of law enforcement workers, for example, had to learn to accept the hardships imposed by their husbands' occupations and to rely on their own initiative and judgment in family matters. They learned to keep busy in a variety of ways, to rationalize their difficulties and, where possible, to seek support among other wives and families of law enforcement personnel (Maynard et al. 1980). The wives of military men who faced frequent or long separations from their husbands also employed similar coping strategies (McCubbin et al. 1978).

The miners' wives, the wives and families of Chesapeake Bay watermen (fishermen), and some groups of Newfoundland fishermen shared other similarities as well. All were a part of families and communities where, throughout their histories, hard work, suffering, self-reliance, and deep pride of heritage were in frequent confrontation with the oppression of both natural and social forces. They lived in relative geographic and social isolation, and they shared generations-old working and social traditions.

The hazards and difficulties of the work of mining, fishing, crabbing, and oystering combined with these geographic and social conditions to create lifestyles in which self-reliance, the maintenance of strong support among family and friends, acceptance of the demands of the work that earned the family's living, and a strong attachment to church and faith were fundamental (Davis 1989, 1983; Ellis 1986; Peffer 1979; Wolf 1986).

Like the miners' wives, the Chesapeake Bay and Newfoundland women could never be sure their husbands would return to them at the end of the fishermen's day or at the end of several weeks' stay at the fishing grounds. Coping with the conditions of their lives was a struggle, and the relationship of these conditions to emotional and physical discomforts was recognized. They "had it hard" (Davis 1983, 73), but worry and anxiety over their husbands' safety was an integral part of their married life; and being able to accept the situation and continue to carry out their responsibilities as wives and mothers was a matter of pride (Davis 1989, 1983; Peffer 1979; Wolf 1986).

In general, the miners' wives and other women whose husbands work in dangerous occupations or on rotating shifts share some similar problems and experiences. They have in common their frequent worry over the hazards of their husbands' jobs and the need to cope constantly with the multiple problems of shift work. They must struggle with the same complex family problems that arise from shift work, and they experience similar emotional consequences from their stresses and strains. If they choose to accept their husbands' occupations rather than persuade them to change occupations, they also have in common the limited availability of effective coping methods.

Despite the common experiences, however, the differences between the miners' wives and many other women appear to be more numerous than the similarities. The miners' wives believe that few other women are so deeply involved in the history, the details, and the daily workings of their husbands' occupations or so emotionally involved in the tensions between management, workers, unions, and the politics of industry. They point out the differences between themselves and other women in terms of the limitations and constraints placed on them by their location, their culture, and the scarcity of alternate occupations; and, for the most part, they are accurate in their assessments.

Compared to many industrial, manufacturing, or service workers, the West Virginia miners have few choices of occupation. In any one area, there are often few or no other places to earn a wage that will support a family. Further, the pressure of generations of men who have ended their education early has placed cultural constraints on the miners' ability to continue their education in the hope of finding less hazardous work. These same tendencies in conjunction with a perennially struggling economy have also limited the availability of further education by limiting educational facilities. Moreover, the traditional perceptions of home and family minimize the desirability of leaving the area to find work in less limited circumstances.

It is likely that the combination of geography, culture, location, and economy and their effects on people are not unique in all respects. There are probably other women in other cultures whose lives are shaped by these same pressures. But, in terms of the United States today, the women seem to be correct when they say, "There is no other job like being a miner's wife."

APPENDIX C

Research Methods and Findings

The sampling plan employed the women's friendship networks to obtain respondents for the study. Each woman, beginning with the first, recommended a friend who she thought would be interested in participating in the study. Initial contacts were made by the women, and any new contacts who did not express interest in the project were not included. My early concerns about obtaining a reasonably representative sample of miners' wives of various ages were soon laid to rest as the expanding network of contacts very quickly began to include young, middle-aged, and older women.

While there was always a period of ice breaking at the beginning of an interview, the wives always greeted the interviewers warmly and with considerable interest in what was being done, how it was being done, and whether it might be useful to other women like themselves. Without exception, after the initial period of getting to know one another, the women were open and candid in response to the interviewers' questions, and throughout the lengthy interviews offered useful suggestions and comments.

The interview schedule was semistructured and contained open-ended questions about the women's worries and conflicts, the events that created tension and anxiety, how the women coped with these events, and how they had learned these coping methods (see Appendix D). The interviewers also asked about the views the women held concerning what, or who, determines the events of their lives and life in general and about their predictions for themselves and their families. Finally, at the end of the interviews, the women were asked to provide background demographic information of themselves and their husbands and to bring up any other topics they wished to discuss. All of the information except the postinterview discussions was tape-recorded for later transcription.

The issues raised in the spontaneous, postinterview discussions often focused on the women's ideas and reactions to current political or social events, women's issues such as concepts of equal pay for equal work or job discrimination of various kinds, the ideas and attitudes of young people, and the role of higher educational institutions in their host communities. Comments on these issues were insightful and sharply critical.

The tape-recorded interviews were transcribed and then subjected to a thematic content analysis aimed at identifying themes of stress, coping, and emotional reactions. The choice of open-ended questions and thematic analysis were based on two considerations. The first was that, insofar as I could determine, no previous research had been directed toward the day-to-day effects of mining on the wives and families of the miners. Therefore, the interviews presented a body of potentially useful information concerning stressful situations of various types, the coping responses used to modify these stresses, and the meanings of these stresses and their coping methods for the women's lives. The second consideration was that the nature of the inquiry favored the use of a method of analysis in which a rapport leading to open communication could be established.

The migration data showed that most of the women had migrated only short distances since their birth. Of those born in the state (n = 16), six were at the time living within five miles of their birthplace, five within fifteen miles, and five within fifty miles. Only two of the women were born in another state.

Differences in demographic characteristics (other than expected differences in age and length of marriage) were found in educational levels and number of children (see Table 1). All but two of the respondents had been employed either full or part time outside their homes at some period in their lives, and two older and two younger ones were presently employed full time. Two older and one younger respondent were employed part time although not on a regular weekly basis. Many had previously held a variety of full-time and part-time occupations such as waitress, factory worker, store clerk, office clerk, and secretary and had been employed at these jobs both prior to marriage and after marriage at times when their husbands were unemployed or earning low wages.

The responses to questions concerning problematic situations underscored the realistic hazards of their husbands' work and provided both content and context for the chronic stress experienced by miners' wives. The women's replies suggested that not only did they experience psychological stress arising from the hazards of their husbands' occupations but that many of the everyday problems they had to confront were also a result of the working structure of mining (see Table 2).

Table 1. Demographic Information

Respondents	Mean age	Mean educ. level	Mean years of marriage	Mean age at marriage	Mean number of children
Older (n = 9)	51.5	9.6	31.5	18.3	4.8
Younger (n = 9)	28.6	12.5	8.5	19.3	1.6

Table 2. Problem-Causing Situations
(*Most frequently mentioned situations, by percentage of respondents*)

Respondents	Shift work	Strikes	Persistent worry over husband's safety
Older (n = 9)	88	66	44
Younger (n = 9)	100	88	66
All (n = 18)	94	77	55

The most frequently mentioned situation that led to problems and worry was job related although not hazard related. Alternating shift work or continued night shift work was the most frequently mentioned problem-creating situation and was considered a major problem area by seventeen of the eighteen women. Strikes were considered major problems by fourteen respondents, and worry over husbands' safety was reported as related to both shift work and strikes. It should be noted that while strikes are primarily job related, they are also hazard related: the women believed the frequency of accidents to be greater in the first few weeks following a return to work after a strike. Further, strikes were reported to create serious financial problems as well as emotional tensions for couples during the time husbands were unemployed and unoccupied at home. The intensity of both types of problems increased as strikes lengthened.

The women reported that the problems created by working alternating shifts or frequent night shifts involved the scheduling of home events, the disciplining of children, the absence of the husband during night hours when children were ill, the inaccessibility of husbands during their time at work, and the completion of chores and maintenance around the home.

Ten of the women stated that worry over husbands' safety at work was a persistent and stressful problem; the remainder reported they

Table 3. Feelings Associated with Problem Situations
(*Most frequently mentioned feelings, by percentage of respondents*)

Respondents	Depression	Nervousness	Crying	Feeling trapped
Older (n = 9)	77	33	22	11
Younger (n = 9)	55	77	33	33
All (n = 18)	66	55	27	22

worried about their husbands only some of the time. Among the younger women, six felt their worry was persistent, and three felt they worried only some of the time; among the older group of women, four felt their worry was persistent, and four felt they worried only some of the time.

Occasional worry was induced and persistent worry was increased by specific environmental stimuli that served to focus attention on the dangers of mining. Most frequently mentioned were hearing or speaking of accidents, a husband's late arrival home after work, and having the phone ring at night while the husband was at work. Specific dangers within the work environment reported as particularly troubling were cave-ins, fires, and black lung. Other dangers mentioned were explosions, gas, machinery accidents, and electrocution.

Feelings of worry included nervousness (irritability, tension, et cetera) (ten women); depression (twelve women); crying spells (five women); and the blues and feelings of being trapped (four women). One woman had experienced anxiety attacks, and nearly all reported occasional periods of insomnia and early waking (see Table 3).

The majority of the women believed that engaging in activities was the most effective means of reducing stress and that experience and religious faith were prerequisites for learning to cope. Reported coping methods covered a broad range of activities described as "keeping busy" (see Table 4). Eleven of the women reported keeping busy as the most useful method of coping, three reported prayer as most effective, and three found sitting quietly and reflecting on their situations most helpful. One respondent reported that only professional therapy had been effective. Older women more often mentioned keeping busy at any kind of task as effective. When younger women specified keeping busy, they meant having an outside job, interacting socially with other people, or becoming involved in a hobby. Only younger women mentioned reflecting on their situations as useful. However, it should be noted that descriptions of reflection

Table 4. Coping Strategies
(*Most frequently mentioned effective strategies, by percentage of respondents*)

Respondents	Keeping busy	Reflection	Prayer
Older (n = 9)	66	0	33
Younger (n = 9)	55	33	0
All (n = 18)	61	33	33

indicated that reflection and prayer are similar strategies that differ in form but not in content.

All of the older women and two of the younger women believed religious faith to be a prerequisite to effective coping; two younger women also believed a combination of faith and experience facilitated effective coping. The remainder of the women believed experience in coping, logical explanations of situations, and help and advice from families and friends were essential for effective coping.

In response to questions about sharing home problems with their husbands, eight women reported they promptly brought domestic problems to their husbands' attention, six reported they did so only at special times (e.g., weekends), and four reported they only occasionally brought domestic problems to their husbands' attention. Younger women were more likely to involve their husbands' in domestic problems than older women, and older women were more likely to do so only at special times or on important occasions. It should be noted that women reported handling problems on their own without enlisting the aid of their husbands as a means of reducing their husbands' burden of work and worry. In situations where husbands' support and aid were not available, the women preferred to turn to parents and siblings.

Most of the wives reported that they considered it essential that their husbands put family and home out of mind while at work in order to reduce the danger of accidents caused by inattention or carelessness. Fourteen reported that they attempted to "make up" for the difficulties and stress of their husbands' jobs through various activities such as handling home problems alone, creating a good atmosphere at home prior to their husbands' departure for work, completing housework and child care tasks before their husbands' return from work, and making special clothing or food items for their husbands. Four, however, did not see these activities as effective in reducing husbands'

Table 5. Injuries and/or Deaths from Mining Accidents
Reported injuries or deaths, by percentage of respondents

Respondents	Husband injured	Immediate family member injured or killed	Member of close social network injured or killed
Older (n = 9)	77	55	66
Younger (n = 9)	55	22	66
All (n = 18)	66	38	66

Table 6. Perceived Control over Environment
(Respondents perceived control, by percentage of respondents)

Respondents	Events outside home		Mine accidents		Events pre-determined	
	Some	None	Some	None	Yes	No
Older (n = 9)	55	44	66	33	100	0
Younger (n = 9)	88	11	88	11	44	22
All (n = 18)	71	27	77	22	72	11

stress and felt that miners' wives could not reduce the difficulties of the miners' jobs.

Nearly all of the respondents felt they were familiar with their husbands' work responsibilities and the dangers involved, although opinions varied concerning how comforting this knowledge was (see Table 5). Thirteen of the women reported their husbands daily discussed their jobs while at home including accidents and injuries, and three women reported occasional discussions of work at home. Three older and three younger women reported they did not wish to know very much about their husbands' jobs, particularly about accidents and injuries, and were reluctant to hear work conversations at home. Only a few older and a few younger women felt reassured about their husbands' safety as the result of understanding his work responsibilities.

Fourteen of the women believed that some control over the political and social environment was possible if people actively worked toward that end and that no control was possible without effort (see Table 6). Younger women more often perceived that control over mining accidents was possible, although only three older respondents believed that no control over accidents was possible. All of the older respondents believed that life events were predetermined by God; only four younger respondents shared this belief.

Twelve of the respondents perceived themselves as having experienced considerable change in their attitudes and ideas since their early marriage years. Specific changes mentioned included becoming more independent, more open, more realistic, and less self-centered. Other changes included more involvement with community activities and with other people outside the family, and more understanding of other people. All believed they would continue to grow and develop as they grew older, and only one saw future change as potentially negative rather than positive.

APPENDIX D

The Interview Schedule

I. Questions concerning problem situations and information relative to husband's job
  A. Do situations ever come up that bother you?
    1. What sort of things are they?
    2. Could you describe how they make you feel?
    3. When you're feeling that way, do you do anything to relieve these feelings?
    4. How does that work?
    5. Do you ever turn to other people for help when you have these problems?
    6. Does this usually make you feel better?
  B. How do work situations influence family relationships?
    1. Do you ever talk to your husband about these things?
    2. Does your husband talk about his work or work problems to you?
    3. How much do you know about your husband's job?
    4. How much do you want to know about your husband's job?
    5. How do you "see" your husband's job compared to yours?
    6. How do you think your husband "sees" your job compared to his?
    7. Do you think your husband's job has an effect on events at home?
    8. Do you think events at home have an effect on your husband's job?
    9. Is there anything about your husband's job that bothers you?
    10. Do you think your husband's job affects your children?
    11. Do you do anything to make your husband's job easier?
    12. Does your husband do anything to make your job easier?
    13. Are your friends miners' wives?
II. Questions concerning coping, control, and widowhood
  A. Coping
    1. How do you think you learned to cope with the problems you've mentioned?

   2. Do you feel you were prepared to be a miner's wife?
   3. Is being a wife to a miner more difficult than being wife to someone in another type of job?
   4. Have your ideas about being a miner's wife changed since you were first married?
   B. What do you think causes things to happen, to go right or wrong?
      1. Outside the home?
      2. On the job?
      3. How much control do you think you have over these events at home? in the community? the state? the nation?
      4. Do you think certain things are supposed to happen to certain people?
      5. Do you believe there is a pattern to people's lives?
   C. Widowhood
      1. Have you ever thought about being a widow?
      2. Have you discussed these thoughts with your husband?
      3. Have you planned what you will do if anything happens to your husband?
      4. Do you have any friends or acquaintances who are widows?
III. Questions concerning development
   A. The future
      1. In the future, do you think you will change very much? Why/why not?
      2. In general, have your ideas about yourself, your life, events in the community or state changed very much over the past ten years? twenty years?
      3. What do you think caused them to change?
      4. How would you say that they have changed?
IV. General questions
   A. What do you think about women working in the mines?
   B. How do you go about solving everyday problems?
   C. Has the way you solve problems changed over time?
 V. Demographic questions
      1. Age?
      2. Education?
      3. Birthplace?
      4. Number of different residences prior to marriage?
      5. Location of immediate relatives?
      6. Number of marriages?
      7. Number of years in current marriage?
      8. Age at first marriage?

9. Length of current marriage? Number of children? ages? sex?
10. Employment before marriage? at present?
    a. types of jobs held? how long?
    b. preferred occupation?
11. Why employed?
12. Years husband has been employed in the mines?
13. Types of mining jobs?
14. Other employment (husband)?
15. Rent or own home?
16. Years in present home?
17. Type of home?
18. Preferred location for home?
19. Reason for preferred location?

References

Akerstedt, Torbjorn. 1988. "Sleepiness as a Consequence of Shift Work." *Sleep* 11(1): 17–34.

Althouse, Robert. 1974. *Work, Safety, and Life Style among Southern Appalachian Coal Miners: A Survey of the Men of Standard Mines.* Morgantown: West Virginia University.

Appalachian Consortium. 1981. *Appalachia America.* Johnson City, Tenn.: East Tennessee Univ. Press.

Arble, Mead. 1976. *The Long Tunnel: A Coal Miner's Journal.* New York: Atheneum.

Brooks, Gwen. 1973. "I Am a Union Woman." In Jim Axelrod, ed., *Growin' Up Country.* Clintwood, Va.: Resource and Information Center, Council of the Southern Mountains.

Caudill, Harry. 1973. "The Mountain, the Miner, and the Lord." In Jim Axelrod, ed., *Growin' Up Country.* Clintwood, Va.: Resource and Information Center, Council of the Southern Mountains.

Coles, Robert. 1971. *Children of Crisis,* vol. 3. New York: Atlantic Monthly Press.

Corbin, David. 1981. *Life, Work, and Rebellion in the Coal Fields: The Southern West Virginia Miners, 1880–1922.* Urbana: Univ. of Illinois Press.

Coward, Raymond, and Robert Jackson.1983. "Environmental Stress: The Rural Family." In Hamilton McCubbin and Charles Figley, eds., *Stress and the Family: Coping with Normative Transitions,* vol. 1 New York: Bruner/Mazel.

Davis, Dona 1983. *Blood and Nerves: The Ethnographic Focus on Menopause.* St John's, Newfoundland: Institute of Social and Economic Research.

Davis, Dona. 1989. "The Variable Character of Nerves in a Newfoundland Fishing Village." *Medical Anthropology vol. 11*: 63–78.

Dunham, Randall. 1979. *Community Structure and the Experiences of Shift Workers.* Springfield, Va.: National Technical Information Service.

Elliott, Michael, Ronald Bingham, Swen Nielsen, and Paul Warner. 1986. "Marital Intimacy and Satisfaction as a Support System for Coping with Police Officer Stress." *Journal of Police Science and Administration* 14(1):40–44.

Ellis, Carolyn. 1986. *Fisher Folk: Two Communities on Chesapeake Bay.* Lexington: Univ. Press of Kentucky.

Finn, Peter. 1981. "The Effects of Shift Work on the Lives of Employees." *Monthly Labor Review* 104(10): 31–35.

Hageman, Mary. 1978. "Occupational Stress and Marital Relationships." *Journal of Police Science and Administration* 6(4):402–12.

Knipe, Edward and Helen Lewis. 1971. "The Impact of Coal Mining on the Traditional Mountain Subculture." In John Morland, ed., *The Not So Solid South: Anthropological Studies in a Regional Subculture.* Athens: Univ. of Georgia Press.

Lewis, Helen, Sue Kobak, and Linda Johnson. 1973. "Family, Religion, and Colonialism in Central Appalachia: Bury My Rifle at Big Stone Gap." In Jim Axelrod, ed., *Growin' up Country.* Clintwood, Va.: Resources and Information Center, Council of the Southern Mountains.

Maggard, Sally. 1990a. "Gender Contested: Women's Participation in the Brookside Coal Strike." In Guida West and Rhoda Blumberg, eds., *Women and Social Protest.* New York: Oxford Univ. Press.

———. 1990b. "Schooling, Work Experience, and Gender: The Social Reproduction of Poverty in Mining Regions. "Paper presented at the Conference on Structural Changes and Regional Development, Hungarian Academy of Sciences, Pecs, Hungary.

Maynard, Peter, Nancy Maynard, Hamilton McCubbin, and David Shao. 1980. "Family Life and the Police Profession: Coping Patterns Wives Employ in Managing Job Stress and the Family Environment." *Family Relations* 29(4):495–501.

Maynard, Peter and Nancy Maynard. 1982. "Stress in Police Families: Some Policy Implications." *Journal of Police Science and Administration* 10(2):302–14.

McCubbin, Hamilton, Pauline Boss, Gary Lester, Jeff Grant, Carol Gordon, James Johnson, and Yvonne Kilkelly. 1978. "Family Coping and Adaptation to Stress." Paper presented at the International Sociological Association, Minneapolis.

Mellor, Earl. 1986. "Shift Work and Flextime: How Prevalent Are They?" *Monthly Labor Review* 109(11):14–21.

Naughton, Jim 1988. "Matewan." *Appalachian Journal* 15(3):218–19.

Painter, Jacqueline. 1987. *The Season of Dorland-Bell: History of an Appalachian School.* Asheville, N.C.: J.B. Painter.

Pearlin, Leonard. 1980. "Life Strains and Psychological Stress: A Conceptual Overview." In Erik Erikson and Neal Smelser, eds., *Themes of Love and Work in Adulthood.* Cambridge: Harvard Univ. Press.

Pearlin, Leonard and M. Lieberman. 1978. "Social Sources of Emotional Distress." In Roberta Simmons, ed., *Research in Community and Mental Health.* Greenwich, Conn.: JAI Press.

Pearlin, Leonard and Carmi Schooler. 1978. "The Structure of Coping." *Journal of Health and Social Behavior* (March):2–21.

Peffer, Randall. 1979. *Watermen.* Baltimore: Johns Hopkins Univ. Press.

Portner, Joyce. 1983. "Work and Family: Achieving a Balance." In Hamilton McCubbin and Charles Figley, eds., *Stress and the Family: Coping with Normative Transitions,* vol. 1. New York: Bruner and Mazel.

Schwartz, Jeffery, and Cynthia Schwartz. 1975. "The Personal Problems of the Police Officer: A Plea for Action." In *Job Stress and the Police Officer: Identifying Stress Reductions Techniques,* Cincinnati: United States Public Health Service.

Scott, Shaunna. 1988. "Where There Is No Middle Ground: Community and Class Consciousness In Harlan County, Kentucky." Ph.D.diss., Univ. of Kentucky.

Simon, Barbara. 1990. "Impact of Shift Work on Individuals and Families." *Families in Society* 71(6):342–45.

Smith, Barbara. 1987. *Digging Our Own Graves.* Philadelphia: Temple Univ. Press.

State of West Virginia. 1986. *Annual Report and Directory of Mines.* Department of Energy, Division of Mines and Minerals. Charleston.

———. 1988. *Annual Report and Directory of Mines.* Department of Energy, Division of Mines and Minerals. Charleston.

Van Maanen, John. 1988. *Tales of the Field: On Writing Ethnography.* Chicago: Univ. of Chicago Press.

Walker, Adelaide. 1932. "Living Conditions in the Coal Fields." In *Harlan Miners Speak: Report on Terrorism in the Kentucky Coal Fields.* Members of the National Committee for the Defense of Political Prisoners. New York: Harcourt, Brace.

Whitehead, John, III. 1979. *The Watermen of the Chesapeake.* Centreville, Md.: Tidewater.

Witt, Matthew, and Earl Dotter. 1979. *In Our Blood.* New Market, Tenn.: Highlander Research and Education Center.

Wolf, Bernard 1986. *Amazing Grace: Smith Island and the Chesapeake Watermen.* New York: Macmillan.

Index

Note: Study subjects are indexed by pseudonym.

portrait of, 137–38; worries about dangers, 49–50, 103

Naughton, Jim, 77, 113

nervousness, as stress symptom, 101, 103, 153

noise in mines, and dangers, 44

older wives: coping strategies of, 110; and education, 23–24, 25; on employment, 29–31; personal portraits of, 140–43

Painter, Jacqueline, 24

panic (anxiety) attacks, 11, 153

Paula (study subject): on changes in herself, 123, 133–34; coping strategies of, 32, 95–96; education of, 71, 138; employment of, 81, 95; on foremen/supervisors, 116–17; and inequality in family responsibilities, 71; personal portrait of, 138; and shift work, 32

Pearlin, Leonard, 90, 105

Peffer, Randall, 147, 148

pneumoconiosis (black lung disease), 3, 10, 51, 56–60, 142, 153

political system, wives' opinions on, 5, 124, 135, 137, 142

Portner, Joyce, 33, 113

prayer, in coping with worry, 100, 104, 108, 153

rationalization, as coping strategy, 93–96

reflection, in coping strategies, 153–54

regulation and regulators, mining, 2, 118, 119

religious activities/beliefs: in coping with worry, 11, 35–36, 56, 97–101, 104, 108, 126, 140, 153, 154; for social support, 21; and widowhood, 53. See also God's will (fate, determination)

roof collapse in mines, 9, 42, 48, 49, 52, 153

Rose (study subject): coping strategies of, 32, 100; employment of, 28, 30, 80; personal portrait of, 140–41; and shift work, 32, 68, 69–70; valuing of self by, 38, 135; worries about dangers, 69–70, 117

routines, in coping strategies, 35–36

safety. See danger; worry, danger-related

Schooler, Carmi, 90, 105

Schwartz, Cynthia, 68, 144, 145

Schwartz, Jeffery, 68, 144, 145

Scott, Shaunna, 12, 13, 14, 16, 17, 22, 23, 40, 44, 45, 64, 76, 97, 113, 120, 147

self-change/growth, 122–23, 124–25, 133–34, 156

self-valuing, 38, 137, 138, 140

Sharon (study subject): activism by, 134; on changes in herself, 125; coping strategies of, 98; on education, 24; employment of, 82; friendships of, 21; and shift work, 31

shift work: and children, 9, 31, 32, 33, 67, 69, 152; coping strategies with, 31–32, 67–69; and danger, 9, 33–34, 44, 69–70, 102, 145, 146; description of specific cases, 31–35, 67–70; and family conflict, 9, 34–35; and family relationships, 9, 32–33, 67, 68, 145–46; and home-making, 9, 31–33, 67–69, 152; in non-mining occupations, 144–46, 148; and social activities, 9, 31, 33, 69; study results summarized, 152; and worry about danger, 8–9, 33–34, 69–70, 102, 152

Simon, Barbara, 144, 145

sleep disturbances, 11, 101, 147, 153

Smith, Barbara, 57

social activities: and extended family,